GUINNESS WORLD RECORDS

50 States

Carson-Dellosa Publishing, LLC
Greensboro, North Carolina

GUINNESS WORLD RECORDS DISCLAIMER: Guinness World Records Limited has a very thorough accreditation system for records verification. However, while every effort is made to ensure accuracy, Guinness World Records Limited cannot be held responsible for any errors contained in this work. Feedback from our readers on any point of accuracy is always welcome.

SAFETY DISCLAIMER: Attempting to break records or set new records can be dangerous. Appropriate advice should be taken first, and all record attempts are undertaken entirely at the participant's risk. In no circumstances will Guinness World Records Limited or Carson-Dellosa Publishing, LLC, have any liability for death or injury suffered in any record attempts. Guinness World Records Limited has complete discretion over whether to include any particular records in the annual Guinness World Records book.

Quarter-dollar coin images from the United States Mint.
Carson-Dellosa Publishing and Guinness World Records Limited are not affiliated with the United States Mint.

Due to the publication date, the facts and the figures contained in this book are current as of January 2012.

© 2013 Guinness World Records Limited

Visit Guinness World Records at *guinnessworldrecords.com*.

Visit *carsondellosa.com* for correlations to Common Core State, national, and Canadian provincial standards.

Credits
Content Editor: Christine Schwab

Carson-Dellosa Publishing, LLC
PO Box 35665
Greensboro, NC 27425 USA
carsondellosa.com

ISBN 978-1-60996-946-2

Table of Contents

Introduction 4
Setting Guinness World Records Records ... 5
United States Map, Labeled 6
United States Map, Blank 7

Alabama 8
Alaska 10
Arizona 12
Arkansas 14
California 16
Colorado 18
Connecticut 20
Delaware 22
Florida 24
Georgia 26
Hawaii 28
Idaho 30
Illinois 32
Indiana 34
Iowa 36
Kansas 38
Kentucky 40
Louisiana 42
Maine 44
Maryland 46
Massachusetts 48
Michigan 50
Minnesota 52
Mississippi 54
Missouri 56
Montana 58
Nebraska 60
Nevada 62
New Hampshire 64
New Jersey 66
New Mexico 68
New York 70
North Carolina 72
North Dakota 74
Ohio 76
Oklahoma 78
Oregon 80
Pennsylvania 82
Rhode Island 84

South Carolina 86
South Dakota 88
Tennessee 90
Texas 92
Utah 94
Vermont 96
Virginia 98
Washington 100
West Virginia 102
Wisconsin 104
Wyoming 106
Washington, DC 108
Abbreviate Those States! 110
United States Word Search 111
Going Crossword Crazy! 112
Riddles Across the USA 114
American Borders 119
Temperature Trends 120
License Plate Fun 121
State Abbreviations Word Fun 122
Design Your Own State Quarter 123
Which State Quarter Is It? 124

Answer Key 125

About This Book

Guinness World Records 50 States teaches students about the United States and Washington, DC, by presenting facts with a fresh, exciting twist! Imagine the spike of interest when students read about a 319-pound hamburger on a restaurant menu in Michigan or a man in Ohio who wore 131 neckties at once. Or, how about when students learn that Kentucky is home to the world's Smallest Dog that stands at merely four inches tall or that a man from Alabama blew a 20-inch bubble gum bubble? Amazing records such as these, along with state facts and puzzles, will have students excited to learn more about the United States!

How This Book Works

World Records: The states are presented in alphabetical order, making it easy to select states to study. Each state's pages highlight a Guinness World Records record that was set in that state. A photograph further documents the record-setting or record-breaking accomplishment.

State Quarters: Below each world record is information about the state's unique quarter. The United States Mint in its 50 State Quarters® Program released five new state quarters for each of 10 years. In 1999, the United States Mint struck five new quarters for the first five states to enter the union: Delaware, Pennsylvania, New Jersey, Georgia, and Connecticut. In 2000, they issued a new quarter for each of the next five states to enter the union. This continued through 2008.

State Facts: Interesting facts such as state's "birthday," nickname, and state symbols are included for each state. Students will also enjoy learning other interesting state statistics such as how many amusement parks, toy stores, and pet and pet supply stores are in their own and other states.

Puzzles: On the book's facing pages are puzzles that will allow students to exercise their critical thinking skills, test their ability to recall, and sharpen their research skills. Activities include crossword puzzles, fact matching, word searches, mystery codes, and more. Plus, the book includes bonus pages of mixed review. For the more challenging activities, feel free to encourage students to use dictionaries, textbooks, and safe online reference sites as needed.

Guinness World Records accomplishments are facts or events that belong in one of eight categories:

Human Body
Amazing Feats
Natural World
Science and Technology
Arts and Media
Modern Technology
Travel and Transport
Sports and Games

Some records are new because they are exciting and involve events that have never been attempted before. People with unique talents or features are also permitted to become record setters. However, most of the records are already established, and people try to find records that they can break. One record holder, Ashrita Furman, has broken or set more than 300 records since 1979.

Guinness World Records receives more than 60,000 requests each year. Record setters and record breakers must apply first so that their attempts are official. The organization sets guidelines for each event to make sure that it can be properly measured. Guinness World Records also makes sure that all record breakers follow the same steps so that each participant gets an equal chance. Professional judges make sure that the guidelines are followed correctly and measured accurately. However, the guidelines may designate other community members who can serve as judges to witness an event. Once the record attempt is approved, the participant gets a framed certificate. The person's name may also be included in the yearly publication or on the Guinness World Records website at *guinnessworldrecords.com*.

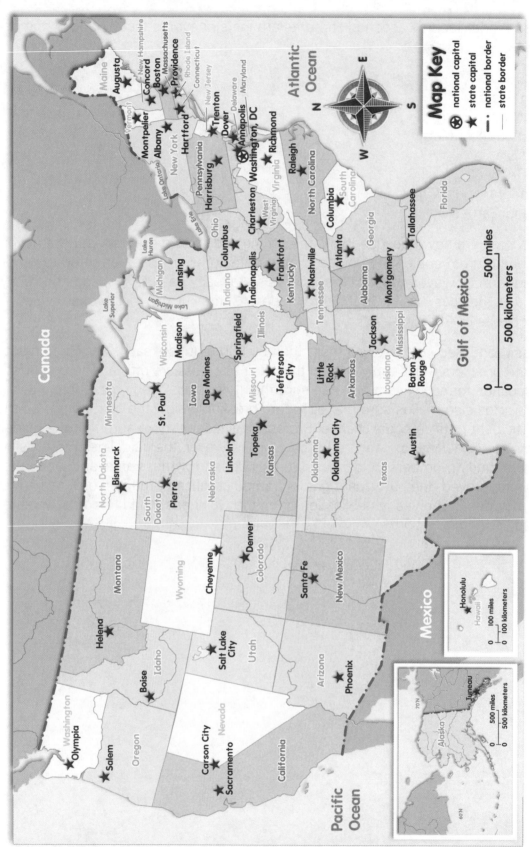

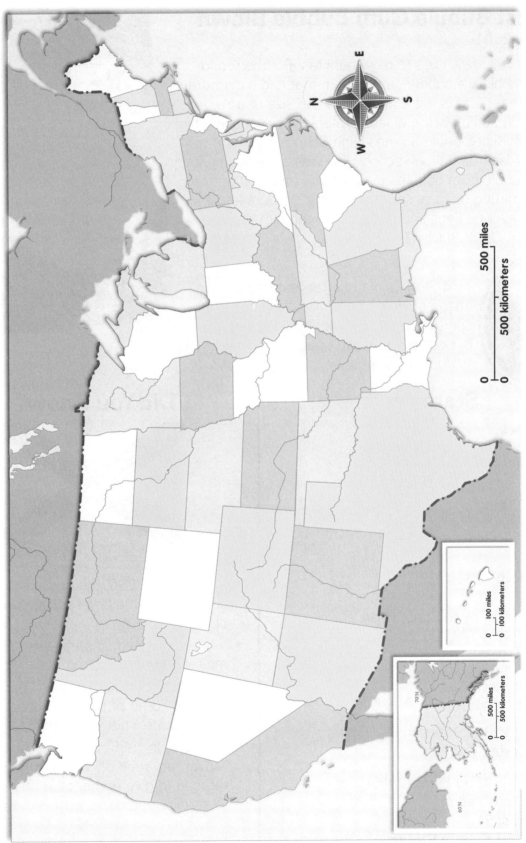

Largest Bubble Gum Bubble Blown
April 24, 2004

Chad Fell really likes to blow bubbles. For the world record, he blew a bubble gum bubble that had a diameter of 20 inches. That is more than twice the size of a basketball! Fell blew the gigantic bubble without using his hands while at Double Springs High School in Winston County, Alabama. In high school, Fell was already blowing bigger bubble gum bubbles than anyone else. Later, while reporting on local sports, he blew big bubbles at sporting events. Fans and players cheered him on. They called him "Bubble Man."

The Alabama quarter features an image of Helen Keller, who defined the spirit of courage. Keller could not see or hear, but she courageously learned to do many things well.

State Facts

Alabama

★ Montgomery

Statehood: 12/14/1819
Rank: 22
Nicknames: Cotton State, Heart of Dixie
Population: 4,779,736 (2010)
State Flower: Camellia
State Bird: Yellowhammer
State Tree: Southern longleaf pine
State Song: "Alabama"
Motto: *We Dare Maintain Our Rights*
Postal Code: AL

Fun Facts (2009)
Amusement Parks: 7
Toy Stores: 81
Pet and Pet Supply Stores: 82

Did You Know?

Alabama
- is where, in 1886, the first electric streetcars in the United States began operating.
- rates cotton and soybeans as some of its main cash crops.
- is called the "Heart of Dixie" because it was the home of the first capital of the Confederate States of America.
- is where, in 1955, the Civil Rights Movement took off when Rosa Parks refused to give up her seat on a city bus to a white person.

Read the clues. Circle the answers in the word search below.

Across

★ the capital of Alabama

★ the name of the city near Russell Cave

★ crop grown in Alabama

★ General Jackson's first name

Down

★ the state flower

★ the city that had the first major civil rights protest

```
F  G  C  X  Y  C  L  E  A  N  D  R  E  W
B  A  A  H  M  C  W  P  S  H  O  P  Z  T
T  S  M  Y  W  Z  A  R  Q  E  A  S  L  T
P  E  E  X  M  O  N  T  G  O  M  E  R  Y
A  Q  L  K  G  H  D  T  Z  Y  X  L  W  B
E  X  L  K  M  B  R  O  I  B  C  M  X  F
B  R  I  D  G  E  P  O  R  T  Y  A  N  V
Y  P  A  W  B  X  W  D  C  O  T  T  O  N
```

Unscramble the circled letters to find the name of the first settlement in Alabama.

_ _ _ _ _ _ _ _

Famous Alabamans

- Coretta Scott King was a civil rights leader and the widow of Martin Luther King Jr.
- Hank Aaron hit more home runs than any other baseball player for two decades.
- Nat "King" Cole was a popular singer.
- Helen Keller, although blind and deaf, became a public speaker and an author.
- Rosa Parks was a civil rights activist who refused to give up her seat to a white person on a city bus.
- Jesse Owens was an Olympic gold medal winner in track and field.
- Harper Lee wrote a novel and won a Pulitzer Prize.

State Greats

- Russell Cave, near Bridgeport, is a national monument. People lived in the cave more than 9,000 years ago.
- NASA's first headquarters was in Huntsville, Alabama.
- Montgomery, Alabama, was the site of Rosa Parks' civil rights protest of the 1960s.
- In 1881, Booker T. Washington was hired at Tuskegee University for African American students.
- The Tenn-Tom Waterway links the Tennessee and Tombigbee rivers. The project moved more dirt than the building of the Panama Canal, a large waterway connecting the Atlantic and Pacific oceans.

Alaska

Fastest Time to Complete the Iditarod Trail
March 15, 2011

The annual Iditarod sled-dog race is held on a trail that was once a mail-supply route. In 1925, a team of mushers and their dogs traveled this trail to take lifesaving medicine to children. The record for fastest time to complete the 1,049-mile Iditarod Trail sled-dog race across Alaska is 8 days, 18 hours, 46 minutes, and 39 seconds. John Baker, who set the record, became the first Alaska native to win the annual race since 1976.

Featured on the Alaska quarter is an image of a brown bear catching a salmon under the North Star. The name Alaska comes from an Aleutian word that means "The Great Land."

State Facts

Statehood: 1/3/1959
Rank: 49
Nicknames: Last Frontier, Great Land, Land of the Midnight Sun
Population: 710,231 (2010)
State Flower: Forget-me-not
State Bird: Willow ptarmigan
State Tree: Sitka spruce
State Song: "Alaska's Flag"
Motto: *North to the Future*
Postal Code: AK

Fun Facts (2009)
Amusement Parks: 2
Toy Stores: 34
Pet and Pet Supply Stores: 19

Did You Know?

Alaska
- is home to Mount McKinley, the highest point in North America.
- is home to Point Barrow, the northernmost point in the United States.
- is the largest of America's states.
- is only 50 miles from Russia at its westernmost point.
- shares a border with no other states in the United States.
- was once called "Seward's Folly" because many people thought Secretary of State William H. Seward was wasting America's money when he bought Alaska.

Use the words in the Word Bank to find and circle words about Alaska in the word search below.

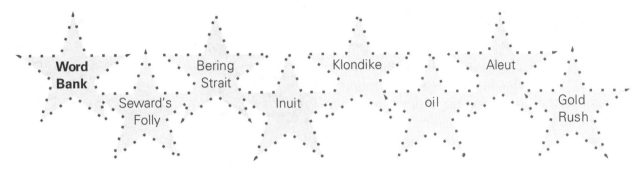

Word Bank

Bering Strait
Klondike
Aleut
Seward's Folly
Inuit
oil
Gold Rush

K	B	T	N	I	A	O	I	L	H	J	Z
L	E	A	N	U	M	K	X	L	S	A	M
O	B	U	K	T	U	E	L	A	U	K	L
T	I	A	R	T	S	G	N	I	R	E	B
T	D	F	O	L	I	A	O	T	D	M	O
S	E	W	A	R	D	S	F	O	L	L	Y
G	O	L	W	E	K	I	D	N	O	L	K
Y	D	H	B	G	O	H	S	U	G	K	D

Famous Alaskans

- William Egan was the first elected governor of Alaska.
- Benny Benson, at 13 years old, designed the state flag.
- Elizabeth Peratrovich supported and worked to pass Alaska's Anti-Discrimination Act.
- Mary Antisarlook protected and herded reindeer.
- Chief Kowee found the first gold at Juneau.
- Edward Lewis "Bob" Bartlett was the first state senator from Alaska.
- Ernest Gruening is known as "the father of Alaskan statehood."

State Greats

- Alaska has more coastline than all of the other states combined.
- Mount McKinley, in Denali National Park, is the highest mountain in North America.
- Point Barrow is the United States' most northern point.
- Alaska also contains Amatignak Island and Semisopochnoi Island, the westernmost and easternmost points in the United States. Both islands are in the Aleutian Islands chain.
- The Trans-Alaska Pipeline takes oil from Prudhoe Bay across Alaska to the port of Valdez.

Largest Gathering of Major Telescopes
2008

After the telescope was invented in the 1600s, it became much easier to study space. The Largest Gathering of Major Telescopes is located at the Kitt Peak National Observatory in Arizona. Kitt Peak is a 6,876-foot mountain with excellent observation conditions and atmospheric clarity. To date, 24 major telescopes and two radio telescopes have been built on its summit since 1958. Kitt Peak is located on the Tohono O'odham Reservation near Tucson.

The Arizona quarter features images of two of the state's most popular attractions: the saguaro cactus and the Grand Canyon. The Grand Canyon became a national park in 1919.

State Facts

Arizona

Phoenix

Statehood: February 14, 1912
Rank: 48
Nickname: Grand Canyon State
Population: 6,482,505 (2011)
State Flower: Saguaro cactus blossom
State Bird: Cactus wren
State Tree: Palo verde
State Song: "Arizona"
Motto: *God Enriches*
Postal code: AZ

Fun Facts (2009)
Amusement Parks: 10
Toy Stores: 166
Pet and Pet Supply Stores: 190

Did You Know?

Arizona
- is where, in 1150, the Hopi people built the village now called Old Oraibi.
- is where, in 1888, the first organized rodeo took place.
- was once part of Mexico.
- is the new home of the London Bridge, which was taken apart, brought to the United States, and reconstructed in the desert.
- is the location of the Grand Canyon.

Draw lines from a blue star to a red star to match the Arizona-related words with their definitions. Each time you make a match, the line should cross out a letter. You may cross out a letter more than once.

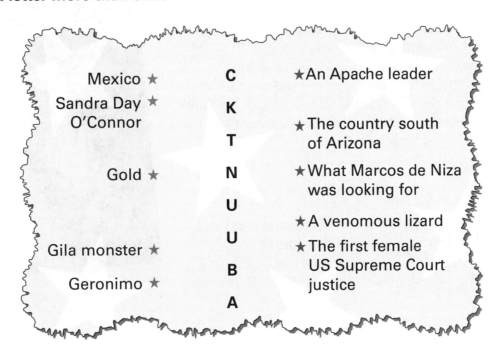

Mexico ★
Sandra Day ★ O'Connor

Gold ★

Gila monster ★

Geronimo ★

C
K
T
N
U
U
B
A

★An Apache leader

★The country south of Arizona

★What Marcos de Niza was looking for

★A venomous lizard

★The first female US Supreme Court justice

You should have five letters left. Unscramble the five letters to find where the first white settlement was built in Arizona.

_____ _____ _____ _____ _____

Famous Arizonans

- Charles D. Poston served in Congress and worked to make Arizona a territory. He is called "the father of Arizona."
- Geronimo was an Apache leader who died at Fort Sill, Oklahoma.
- Chief Cochise was another Apache leader. He was never captured.
- Wyatt Earp was the deputy US marshal at Tombstone.
- Bill Williams was a settler who lived with the Osaga tribe.
- Sandra Day O'Connor was Arizona's assistant attorney general and became the first woman Supreme Court justice.

State Greats

- Hopi Village, on the Hopi Indian Reservation, is the oldest village in the United States.
- The Gila monster that lives in Arizona's deserts is the only venomous lizard found in the United States.
- The Grand Canyon is the largest canyon in the United States.
- The Sonoran Desert is one of the hottest places in the United States. Summer temperatures average 103 degrees Fahrenheit.
- The Hoover Dam is one of the largest hydroelectric plants in the United States. It was named after President Herbert Hoover.

Arkansas

Rarest Bird

Listen! Do you hear a *rap-rap* tapping sound? Is it a woodpecker? If you happen to see a beautiful black-and-white woodpecker with a red crest on its head, pay close attention. The North American ivory-billed woodpecker is currently the world's rarest and most endangered bird. It was thought to be extinct until a single male was seen in both the Cache River and White River national wildlife refuges of Arkansas. If others exist, they haven't been seen by human eyes for a long time.

The Arkansas quarter features images of a duck, a rice stalk, and a diamond, three of the state's many natural resources. Diamond mine visitors may keep what they find!

State Facts

Arkansas
Little Rock ★

Statehood: 6/15/1836
Rank: 25
Nicknames: The Natural State, Land of Opportunity, Wonder State
Population: 2,915,918 (2010)
State Flower: Apple blossom
State Bird: Mockingbird
State Tree: Pine
State Song: "Oh, Arkansas"
Motto: *The People Rule*
Postal Code: AR

Fun Facts (2009)
Amusement Parks: 3
Toy Stores: 65
Pet and Pet Supply Stores: 39

Did You Know?

Arkansas

- is nicknamed the "Land of Opportunity."
- borders the Mississippi River along its eastern flank.
- was part of the huge land parcel known as the Louisiana Purchase.
- is the birthplace of Bill Clinton, the forty-second president, who was its governor.
- was visited in 1541 by Spanish explorer Hernando de Soto, who was the first European to see it.

Read the clues and unscramble the words. Then, find and circle them in the word search below.

★ President Clinton's first name   LBIL   — — — —

★ A national river   FFULBOA   — — — — — — —

★ An explorer of Arkansas   LLLAASE   — —   — — — — —

★ Founder of Arkansas Post   TINTO   — — — — —

★ President Clinton's hometown   EOPH   — — — —

★ A writer who lives in Stamps   AAYM   — — — —

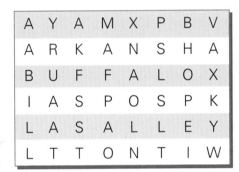

A	Y	A	M	X	P	B	V
A	R	K	A	N	S	H	A
B	U	F	F	A	L	O	X
I	A	S	P	O	S	P	K
L	A	S	A	L	L	E	Y
L	T	T	O	N	T	I	W

Now, use some of the leftover letters to write the name of the first village in Arkansas.

— — — — — — — —   — — — —

Famous Arkansans

- William Jefferson Clinton was born in Hope, Arkansas, and became the forty-second president of the United States.
- Maya Angelou is a writer who often writes about her home in Stamps, Arkansas.
- Douglas MacArthur was an important military leader during World War II.
- Sam M. Walton founded the Wal-Mart stores.
- Hattie Ophelia Wyatt Caraway was the first woman elected to the US Senate.
- William Grant Still was the first African American to conduct an American professional symphony.

State Greats

- The Buffalo River was the United States' first national river.
- Crater of Diamonds State Park, near Murfreesboro, is the only diamond mine in North America open to the public.
- The University of Arkansas is located in Fayetteville.
- Ozark folk music and crafts entertain tourists at the Ozark Folk Center in Mountain View.
- Mount Magazine is the highest point in the state. It is 2,753 feet above sea level.
- Hot Springs is known for the healing waters of its natural springs.

California

Largest Collection of Banana-Related Memorabilia
February 12, 1999

Ken Bannister is bananas about bananas! Bannister started collecting banana-related objects more than 30 years ago. He has the largest collection in the world. His collection includes plastic bananas, stuffed bananas, banana mugs, banana soaps, banana clocks, banana puppets—you name it. If it looks like a banana, it is probably in Bannister's collection. Bannister's International Banana Club Museum in Altadena, California, displays more than 17,000 banana-related items.

The California quarter features images of an endangered California condor in flight, Yosemite Valley, and John Muir. Congress established Yosemite National Park in 1890.

State Facts

Statehood: 9/9/1850
Rank: 31
Nickname: The Golden State
Population: 37,253,956 (2010)
State Flower: Golden poppy
State Bird: California valley quail
State Tree: California redwood
State Song: "I Love You, California"
Motto: *Eureka (I Have Found It)*
Postal Code: CA

Fun Facts (2009)
Amusement Parks: 49
Toy Stores: 928
Pet and Pet Supply Stores: 1,130

Did You Know?

California
- is the most populated state in the nation.
- was claimed for England in 1579 by Sir Francis Drake.
- belonged to Mexico until 1848.
- is the home of the world's largest living thing, a tree found in Sequoia National Park.
- is the location of Death Valley, the lowest point in North America.
- is the home state of Ronald Reagan, the fortieth president, who was its governor.

Read the clues. Unscramble the words about California.

★ the state flower   YPPOP   __ __ __ __ __

★ the tallest mountain in California   TYHNIWE   __ __ __ __ __ __ __

★ the lowest place in California   EATDH AYLLVE __ __ __ __ __ __ __ __ __ __ __

★ a famous national park   OSMTYEIE   __ __ __ __ __ __ __ __

★ the Spanish built 21 of them   SISMNIOS   __ __ __ __ __ __ __ __

★ the movie capital of the world   LLDOOHYOW   __ __ __ __ __ __ __ __ __

★ the state nickname   OGDLNE   __ __ __ __ __ __

Famous Californians

- Richard Nixon was the thirty-seventh president.
- John Steinbeck was a writer who set most of his novels in California.
- Sally Ride was the first woman in space.
- Shirley Temple Black was a child actress and ambassador to the United Nations.
- General George S. Patton Jr. was a famous military leader during World War II.
- Ronald Reagan was our fortieth president and also governor of California. He had been an actor in films as well.

State Greats

- Disneyland, Walt Disney's first theme park, is located near Los Angeles.
- Hollywood is the movie capital of the world.
- San Francisco is famous for its Golden Gate Bridge.
- Sequoia National Park's giant sequoia trees are the largest living things.
- Yosemite National Park is home to Yosemite Falls, the nation's highest waterfall.
- Death Valley contains the lowest point in the Western Hemisphere.
- Mount Whitney is the highest peak in the United States outside of Alaska.

Most Vertical Feet Uphill in Snowshoes by a Woman in 24 Hours
February 8, 2009

Snowshoes can be fun to walk in with a little practice. It is almost impossible to walk backward in snowshoes. And, it is harder to walk uphill in snowshoes than on level ground. Eileen Wysocki set the record for the most vertical feet snowshoed uphill in 24 hours. She climbed 25,534 feet at the Sunlight Mountain Resort in Glenwood Springs, Colorado.

The Colorado quarter features an image of the craggy Rocky Mountains that span the state. The state's name is derived from a Spanish word that means "colored red."

State Facts

Colorado
★ Denver

Statehood: 8/1/1876
Rank: 38
Nickname: Centennial State
Population: 5,029,196 (2010)
State Flower: White-and-lavender columbine
State Bird: Lark bunting
State Tree: Colorado blue spruce
State Song: "Where the Columbines Grow"
Motto: *Nothing Without the Deity*
Postal Code: CO

Fun Facts (2009)
Amusement Parks: 8
Toy Stores: 213
Pet and Pet Supply Stores: 221

Did You Know?

Colorado
- is a very mountainous state, with the highest average elevation of any state.
- is a great place to search for dinosaur bones.
- is the home of the United States Air Force Academy.
- is the location of the world's highest suspension bridge.
- is where, around AD 750, the Anasazi people built pueblos at Mesa Verde and then lived there for more than 700 years.

Use the words in the word bank to find and circle the words about Colorado in the word search below.

Word Bank

Dempsey   Denver   gold   Mesa

Bates   Pikes Peak   Leadville

R	Y	D	N	A	L	S	U	N	P
M	M	E	O	T	G	O	L	D	I
E	L	N	A	P	D	V	K	E	K
S	E	V	G	B	A	T	E	S	E
A	U	E	O	K	B	H	A	F	S
C	Y	R	R	P	I	G	U	O	P
T	E	W	M	O	S	A	L	D	E
G	V	D	E	M	P	S	E	Y	A
L	E	A	D	V	I	L	L	E	K

Famous Coloradans

- M. Scott Carpenter from Boulder was one of America's first astronauts.
- Patricia Schroeder was the first woman from Colorado elected to Congress.
- Florence Rena Sabin was the first woman named to the National Academy of Sciences.
- William Harrison "Jack" Dempsey was the world heavyweight boxing champion.
- Ouray was a Ute chief.
- Ben Nighthorse Campbell was the first American Indian elected to the US Senate.

State Greats

- Pikes Peak inspired Katharine Lee Bates to write "America the Beautiful" after a hiking trip.
- Colorado Springs is the home of the United States Air Force Academy.
- Skiers from around the world visit Colorado in the winter. The winter population of Vail is up to five times higher on weekends than on weekdays.
- Leadville is the highest city in the United States.
- Dinosaurs once roamed the state of Colorado. Scientists found so many fossils in one area that it was turned into Dinosaur National Monument.

Connecticut

Largest Simultaneous Launch of Sea Kayaks
July 29, 2006

Even if you have never picked up a paddle, it's easy to support Kayak for a Cause. In this event, kayakers come together to cross the Long Island Sound each year for charity. The 2006 event earned the record for the Largest Simultaneous Launch of Sea Kayaks with 303. The kayakers left shore from Calf Pasture Beach in Norwalk, Connecticut, and paddled about 13 miles across the sound to Long Island, New York.

The Connecticut quarter features an image of the Charter Oak tree. Beginning in 1687, the tree provided a hiding place for Connecticut's charter, which was a symbol of liberty.

State Facts

Connecticut

★ Hartford

Statehood: 1/9/1788
Rank: 5
Nicknames: Constitution State, Provision State, Nutmeg State
Population: 3,574,097 (2010)
State Flower: Mountain laurel
State Bird: Robin
State Tree: White oak
State Song: "Yankee Doodle"
Motto: *He Who Transplanted Still Sustains*
Postal Code: CT

Fun Facts (2009)
Amusement Parks: 4
Toy Stores: 116
Pet and Pet Supply Stores: 125

Did You Know?

Connecticut
- is known as the "Constitution State."
- chose "Yankee Doodle" as its state song.
- is a leading producer of helicopters and submarines.
- is the birthplace of mass production manufacturing, thanks to Eli Whitney, inventor of the cotton gin.
- is the home of many American Indian groups such as the Pequot, the Mohegan, and the Niantic.

Complete the crossword puzzle.

Across

1 The man who invented the cotton gin

4 A university located in New Haven

6 The town where the first helicopter was developed in America

Down

2 First name of the author of *Uncle Tom's Cabin*

3 First nuclear-powered submarine

5 He discovered Connecticut

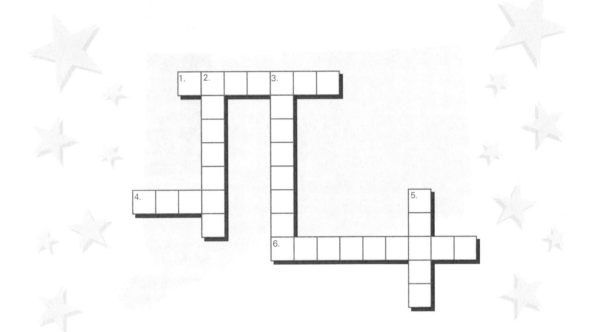

Famous Connecticuters

- Nathan Hale was a Revolutionary War hero.
- Eli Whitney invented the cotton gin.
- Harriet Beecher Stowe wrote *Uncle Tom's Cabin*, a book about slavery.
- Noah Webster gave us our Webster's Dictionary.
- P. T. Barnum called his circus "The Greatest Show on Earth."
- Charles Goodyear developed a process for making rubber.
- Dean Acheson was a senator who helped write the Marshall Plan and the Truman Doctrine.

State Greats

- The first helicopter in America was developed in Stratford in 1939.
- Visitors to Groton can tour the first nuclear-powered submarine, the USS *Nautilus*.
- Yale University, the third oldest university in the nation, is located in New Haven.
- Mystic Seaport is a popular vacation spot.
- Hartford is called "America's Insurance Capital" since the oldest insurance company in the United States is located there.
- Bridgeport is sometimes called "Park City" because it has many open spaces.
- A large hurricane called the "Great Hurricane" hit New London in 1938.

Delaware

Longest Career in the Same Company
2008

Can you imagine working at the same company for 80 years? Most people work at several different companies in their lifetimes. But, Thomas Stoddard (born in 1912) worked at only one company for his entire career. He worked for Speakman Company in Wilmington, Delaware, and set the record for having the Longest Career in the Same Company. When Stoddard retired in 2008, he was 96. Stoddard started working at Speakman in 1928 as a mail boy.

The Delaware quarter features an image of Caesar Rodney, who rode 80 miles through terrible weather to place Delaware's tie-breaking vote in favor of the Declaration of Independence.

State Facts

Delaware
★ Dover

Became a state: 12/7/1787
Rank: 1
Nicknames: First State, Diamond State
Population: 897,934 (2010)
State Flower: Peach blossom
State Bird: Blue hen
State Tree: American holly
State Song: "Our Delaware"
Motto: *Liberty and Independence*
Postal Code: DE

Fun Facts (2009)
Amusement Parks: 4
Toy Stores: 31
Pet and Pet Supply Stores: 40

Did You Know?

DECEMBER 7, 1787

Delaware
- is known as the "First State" because it was first to join the Union.
- is also nicknamed the "Diamond State."
- is named after Thomas West, who was Lord De La Warr.
- is bordered on the east by the Atlantic Ocean.
- is a leading producer of broiler chickens.
- was first seen by a European when Henry Hudson explored it in 1609.

Unscramble the words to complete the sentences.

★ ★

★ Delaware was the ___ ___ ◯ ___ ___ state to enter the Union.   SRFIT

★ ◯◯ ___ ___ ___ is the state capital of Delaware.   OREDV

★ There are two towns that are located on the border of Delaware

 and ___ ___ ___ ◯ ___ ___ ___ ___.   YLNMAARD

★ Richard ___ ___ ___ ◯◯ created the African Methodist Episcopal Church.   EANLL

Rearrange the circled letters to form the name of a Delaware hero.

___ ___ ___ ___ ___ ___

★ ★

Famous Delawarians

- Oliver Evans was an inventor, scientist, and researcher.
- Henry Heimlich developed the "Heimlich maneuver," a method used to help choking victims.
- Annie Jump Cannon discovered 300 stars.
- Frank Stephens began a small community named Arden in 1900.
- Richard Allen created the African Methodist Episcopal Church.
- John Phillips Marquand won the Pulitzer Prize for his novel *The Late George Apley*.

State Greats

- Wilmington is home to the world's second largest maker of chemicals—E. I. du Pont de Nemours and Company.
- Settlers from Holland, Sweden, and England all built settlements along the Delaware River. This is the only area in the country where all three countries built settlements.
- A reproduction of the Town Hall of Hoorn from the Netherlands was built in Lewes.
- Two communities are in both Delaware and Maryland: Delmar and Marydel.
- Delaware is the only state with a rounded border.

Florida

City with the Largest Foreign-Born Population
2001

A big city is often made up of different kinds of people from different places—many even speaking different languages. The city with the highest percentage of people born outside the United States is Miami, Florida. In 2001, 59 percent of about five million Miami residents were people who had been born outside of the United States.

The Florida quarter features images of a Spanish galleon and a US space shuttle flying above a shore lined with palm trees. The images connect Florida to its slogan "Gateway to Discovery."

State Facts

Florida
★ Tallahassee

Statehood: 3/3/1845
Rank: 27
Nicknames: Sunshine State, Peninsula State
Population: 18,801,310 (2010)
State Flower: Orange blossom
State Bird: Mockingbird
State Tree: Sabal palmetto
State Song: "Old Folks at Home"
Motto: *In God We Trust*
Postal Code: FL

Fun Facts (2009)
Amusement Parks: 62
Toy Stores: 474
Pet and Pet Supply Stores: 655

Did You Know?

Florida

- is known as the "Sunshine State."
- has a name that means "feast of flowers" in Spanish.
- is the theme park capital of the world.
- is the location of Saint Augustine, founded in 1565, the oldest city in the United States.
- is a large peninsula; no point in this state is more than 70 miles from open water.
- is the location of the Kennedy Space Center where the space shuttle is launched.

Complete the sentences about Florida.

★ Big reptiles live in the __ __ __ __ __ __ __ __ __ __ .

★ The state flower is the __ __ __ __ __ __ __ __ __ __ __ __ __.

★ Ponce de León was looking for a __ __ __ __ __ __ __ __ of youth when he arrived in Florida.

★ Lake __ __ __ __ __ __ __ __ __ __ is the largest lake in Florida.

★ Tallahassee is Florida's __ __ __ __ __ __ __.

★ Saint __ __ __ __ __ __ __ __ was founded by the Spanish.

Famous Floridians

- Mary McLeod Bethune was a famous African American teacher who later served as a presidential advisor.
- Gloria Estefan is a singer. She used to head a group called the Miami Sound Machine.
- Chris Evert is a tennis player who won Wimbledon in 1974, 1976, and 1981.
- Sidney Poitier is an actor best known for the movie *Guess Who's Coming to Dinner*.
- John Ringling ran a circus, which is still running today.

State Greats

- The Kennedy Space Center launched the first man to land on the moon.
- Disney World, in Orlando, covers 28,000 acres and has Florida's largest hotel with more than 2,800 rooms.
- Most of Florida is less than 100 feet above sea level.
- The Everglades is the only place in the world where crocodiles and alligators live together naturally.
- Florida adopted its sixth and most recent constitution in 1968.

Largest Aquarium
November 2005

Where can you go to see dolphins, otters, butterfly fish, and a beluga whale all in one place? Try the Georgia Aquarium in Atlanta, Georgia. It's the world's Largest Aquarium if you measure the amount of water in it. Its habitats hold a total of 8 million gallons of fresh and salt water. The attraction contains 120,000 fish and animals from 500 different species. The largest of the aquarium's 60 different habitats contains 6.2 million gallons and is home to whale sharks.

Georgia has a quarter that features an image of a peach within an outline of the state. Live oak branches and a banner showing the state's motto frame the peach.

State Facts

Georgia

★Atlanta

Statehood: 1/2/1788
Rank: 4
Nicknames: Peach State, Goober State, Empire State of the South
Population: 9,687,653 (2010)
State Flower: Cherokee rose
State Bird: Brown thrasher
State Tree: Live oak
State Song: "Georgia on My Mind"
Motto: *Wisdom, Justice, and Moderation*
Postal Code: GA

Fun Facts (2009)
Amusement Parks: 11
Toy Stores: 193
Pet and Pet Supply Stores: 192

Did You Know?

Georgia
- is the largest state east of the Mississippi River.
- is the location of Stone Mountain, a popular tourist attraction.
- is the nation's leading producer of peanuts.
- is the birthplace of James (Jimmy) Earl Carter Jr., the thirty-ninth president, who was previously its governor.
- Georgia was named after King George II of England.

Complete the crossword puzzle.

Across

3 Home of Coca-Cola and CNN

5 Famous civil rights leader

6 Peanut farmer and former president

Down

1 Columbus is on the border with this state

2 The first English colony in Georgia

4 This city's name sounds like a summer month

6 One of the greatest baseball players

Famous Georgians

- Jimmy Carter was governor of Georgia and the thirty-ninth president of the United States.
- Ty Cobb was one of the greatest baseball players of all time.
- Martin Luther King Jr. was a civil rights leader. He was assassinated in 1968.
- Elijah Muhammad was a leader of the African American Muslim movement.
- Jackie Robinson was the first African American baseball player in the Major Leagues.
- Flannery O'Connor was a writer whose books include *Wise Blood*.

State Greats

- The first steamship to cross the Atlantic Ocean, the SS *Savannah*, sailed from Savannah to Liverpool, England, in 1819.
- 1.5 billion pounds of peanuts are harvested every year in Georgia.
- A pharmacist named John Stith Pemberton invented Coca-Cola. The first beverage was a different version of today's soft drink. It was first sold as a soda fountain drink for five cents at Jacobs' Pharmacy in Atlanta.
- Georgia is a leading grower of peaches.
- The Girl Scouts was founded by Juliette Gordon Low in Savannah in 1912.

Largest Collection of Surfboards
November 5, 2009

Hawaii is full of surfboards. But, Donald Dettloff has more than any other person in the world with a total of 647! He has been collecting surfboards for more than 15 years. His displayed collection on his property in Haiku, Maui, Hawaii, is often called "the surfboard fence." The surfboard fence started back in 1990. Because a hurricane was expected, Dettloff wired the boards to his fence to keep them from blowing away.

The Hawaii quarter features images of King Kamehameha I and the eight major Hawaiian Islands. The king brought about the unification of the Hawaiian Islands in the early 1800s.

State Facts

Statehood: 8/21/1959
Rank: 50
Nickname: Aloha State
Population: 1,360,301 (2010)
State Flower: Yellow hibiscus brackenridgei
State Bird: Nene
State Tree: Kukui (candlenut)
State Song: "Hawaii Ponoi"
Motto: *The Life of the Land Is Perpetuated in Righteousness*
Postal Code: HI

Fun Facts (2009)
Amusement Parks: 4
Toy Stores: 43
Pet and Pet Supply Stores: 31

Did You Know?

Hawaii
- is the only state not on the mainland of North America.
- is bordered on all sides by the Pacific Ocean.
- is where Pearl Harbor is located; the bombing of the Navy base led to the involvement of the United States in World War II.
- was first ruled by King Kamehameha I.
- is the location of Haleakala, the world's largest dormant (sleeping) volcano.

Use the words in the Word Bank to find and circle the words about Hawaii in the word search below.

Word Bank

Hawaii · pineapple · volcano · Polynesian · aloha · Pearl Harbor · hibiscus · Lanai · Mauna Loa · island · nene · Oahu · flag · canoes

```
S  H  T  M  U  R  B  A  L  F  E  C  G  E  A  I
C  I  A  B  A  O  Q  W  L  A  N  A  I  H  L  S
Y  B  D  W  M  V  E  D  V  E  D  N  D  I  O  L
A  I  F  L  A  G  S  F  O  G  C  O  B  J  H  A
N  S  U  T  U  I  P  O  L  Y  N  E  S  I  A  N
X  C  S  V  N  K  I  J  C  I  H  S  C  A  O  D
M  U  P  E  A  R  L  H  A  R  B  O  R  K  P  B
C  S  R  Q  L  M  L  P  N  E  N  E  O  N  H  F
Z  B  W  L  O  A  H  U  O  U  G  M  J  P  X  L
P  I  N  E  A  P  P  L  E  K  A  Z  G  I  N  Y
```

Famous Hawaiians

- King Kamehameha I formed Hawaii into a peaceful kingdom and expanded trade with other countries.
- Queen Liliuokalani was the last royal leader, her reign ending in 1893.
- Luther Gulick was the founder of the Camp Fire Girls.
- Lois Lowry is a children's author.
- Don Ho was a singer and an entertainer.
- Duke Kahanamoku was a famous Olympic swimmer who made surfing and Hawaiian shirts popular.
- Father Damien, a missionary, worked with people with leprosy (Hansen's disease), even after contracting the disease himself.

State Greats

- The Arizona Memorial floats above where the battleship *Arizona* was sunk on December 7, 1941, during the attack on Pearl Harbor, Oahu.
- Hawaii's Volcanoes National Park contains Mauna Loa, the world's largest active volcano.
- Kauai's Waimea Canyon has brilliantly colored walls and is half a mile deep.
- The Polynesian Cultural Center, on the island of Oahu, has Polynesian music and dance performances. It also has seven reconstructed native villages.
- Diamond Head, an extinct volcano, overlooks famous Waikiki Beach.
- Hawaii is the only state that is made up entirely of islands.

Largest Temporary Straw Bale Maze

October 1, 2011

The Largest Temporary Straw Bale Maze was appropriately named Mega Maze. The huge maze measured 96,847 square feet. Garden Cents, a nursery in Rupert, Idaho, built Mega Maze. The company used several designs, including a 3-D section and a pyramid. The maze, which was made up of 3,202 bales of straw, took three weeks to build. The maze had 1.6 miles of paths running through it. When the fun was over, nearby dairy cows enjoyed using the straw as bedding.

The Idaho quarter features an image of the state raptor, the peregrine falcon, and the state's outline. The state motto shown on the coin means "Let It Be Perpetual."

State Facts

Statehood: 7/3/1890
Rank: 43
Nickname: The Gem State
Population: 1,567,582 (2010)
State Flower: Syringa
State Bird: Mountain bluebird
State Tree: Western white pine
State Song: "Here We Have Idaho"
Motto: *Let It Be Perpetual*
Postal Code: ID

Fun Facts (2009)
Amusement Parks: 6
Toy Stores: 54
Pet and Pet Supply Stores: 39

Did You Know?

Idaho
- is best known for its potatoes.
- is one of the nation's leading producers of silver.
- is the home of Hells Canyon, which is deeper than the Grand Canyon.
- is the home of Lewiston, a Pacific port city that is almost 500 miles inland.
- was explored in 1805 by Lewis and Clark on their Journey of Discovery.
- was home to many American Indians including the Bannock, the Shoshone, the Nez Perce, the Kootenai, the Pen d'Oreille, and the Coeur d'Alene.

Find five names related to the Gem State in the word puzzle below. Some letters are together, but others are mixed up. You will use each box only once. The first letters are already there for you.

EW	L	GL	H	O
L	D	J	I	EA
SA	B	M	O	K
I	U	A	AW	S
C	CA	A	R	R

L _____   C _____

I _____   Sa _____   B _____

Famous Idahoans

- Sacajawea, a Shoshone woman, helped Lewis and Clark explore the Louisiana Territory.
- Moses Alexander became the first Jewish governor in the United States.
- Gutzon Borglum, the artist who designed and sculpted the Mount Rushmore Memorial, was born near Bear Lake, Idaho.
- Lana Turner of Wallace, Idaho, was one of the world's greatest movie stars.
- Carol Ryrie Brink, author of the Newbery Medal–winning book, *Caddie Woodlawn*, was born in Moscow, Idaho.
- Famous poet and author, Ezra Pound, was born in Hailey, Idaho.

State Greats

- Philo Farnsworth invented the television in Rigby, Idaho, in 1922.
- The Amalgamated Sugar Company, the largest sugar refinery in the United States, is in Boise.
- One of the biggest nesting places of hawks and eagles in the United States is at the Snake River Birds of Prey National Conservation Area.
- Arco, Idaho, was the first town in the world that used nuclear energy to generate electricity.

Fastest 100 Meters by a Dog with a Can Balanced on the Head
September 3, 2008

Sweet Pea is a dog that is half collie and half shepherd. She has enjoyed many hours of training with her owner, Alex Rothacker, and holds more than one Guinness World Records record. Sweet Pea set this particular record in Grayslake, Illinois. She walked 100 meters (328 feet) while balancing a can on her head. That is more than the length of an American football field! She did it faster than any other dog and did not drop the can even once. It took her 2 minutes, 55 seconds to set the record. Good girl, Sweet Pea!

The 21 stars on the Illinois quarter symbolize the state's status as the 21st state and its place today in the 21st century. An image of Abraham Lincoln is featured in front of state's outline.

State Facts

Illinois

Springfield ★

Statehood: 12/3/1818
Rank: 21
Nicknames: Land of Lincoln, Prairie State
Population: 12,830,632 (2010)
State Flower: Violet
State Bird: Cardinal
State Tree: White oak
State Song: "Illinois"
Motto: *State Sovereignty, National Union*
Postal Code: IL

Fun Facts (2009)
Amusement Parks: 15
Toy Stores: 336
Pet and Pet Supply Stores: 352

Did You Know?

ILLINOIS

Illinois

- is bordered on the west by the Mississippi River.
- is the home of Sears Tower, one of the world's tallest buildings.
- is the birthplace of Ronald Reagan, the fortieth president.
- is the place where Abraham Lincoln, the sixteenth president, lived most of his life.
- was explored by Jacques Marquette and Louis Joliet in 1673.
- is known as the "Land of Lincoln."

Complete the clues. Then, use the clues to find words in the word search below.

★ Illinois is called the Land of _____ .

★ An American Indian who fought against settlers _____

★ The lake that borders Chicago _____

★ The northernmost large city _____

★ An amusement ride invented in Illinois was the _____ wheel.

★ The state bird of Illinois is the _____ .

```
B   S   I   C   F   F   A   R   D   I   N   A   L   I   N   C
S   L   G   H   N   E   E   N   C   G   O   J   M   S   R   A
F   L   A   H   G   L   R   R   A   L   N   F   I   E   T   R
L   I   N   C   O   L   N   R   R   R   Y   U   C   M   F   D
W   R   O   C   K   F   O   R   D   I   H   I   H   M   G   I
P   C   Q   D   J   H   W   T   I   S   S   Y   I   D   V   N
Q   O   O   Y   H   N   A   E   N   T   G   H   G   K   T   A
B   L   X   S   G   J   I   W   A   G   J   K   A   P   C   L
I   N   R   T   U   K   D   Q   K   D   F   R   N   I   T   S
```

Famous Illinoisans

- Black Hawk was a Sauk American Indian chief. He fought in two wars against American settlers.
- Ernest Hemingway was a world-famous author.
- Jackie Joyner-Kersee was an Olympic champion in the long jump and other track-and-field events.
- Former actor, Ronald Reagan, the fortieth president and governor of California, was the only president born in Illinois.
- Walt Disney created Mickey Mouse and began Disneyland.
- Frank Lloyd Wright was one of America's most famous architects.

State Greats

- The original Ferris wheel was built in Chicago in 1893 by George W. G. Ferris.
- Ronald Reagan spent his early days as a radio announcer for the Chicago Cubs.
- Chicago is known as the "Windy City."
- One of the world's tallest buildings, the Sears Tower, is in Chicago.
- The city of Pekin was named after Peking, China, because an early settler thought it was directly opposite from the Chinese city. It is not.

Longest Tail on a Pony
July 24, 2010

Golden Shante, also known as Topper, is a Shetland pony. Golden Shante holds the record for having the world's Longest Tail on a Pony. Shante's long, blond tail measures 13 feet 5 inches. That is a lot of horsehair! Like Rapunzel's hair in the famous fairy tale, Golden Shante's tail just grew and grew. Judges officially measured Shante's tail at Brookwood Farm in New Palestine, Indiana.

The 19 stars on the Indiana quarter represent the state's status as the 19th state. The race car is featured because of the world-famous Indianapolis 500 race held there each year.

State Facts

Statehood: 12/11/1816
Rank: 19
Nickname: Hoosier State
Population: 6,483,802 (2010)
State Flower: Peony
State Bird: Cardinal
State Tree: Tulip tree
State Song: "On the Banks of the Wabash, Far Away"
Motto: *The Crossroads of America*
Postal Code: IN

Fun Facts (2009)
Amusement Parks: 11
Toy Stores: 171
Pet and Pet Supply Stores: 167

Did You Know?

Indiana
- is called the "Hoosier State" by many people.
- is bordered on the south by the Ohio River.
- is the home of the "Greatest Spectacle in Racing," the Indy 500, an auto race held in its capital city every Memorial Day weekend.
- is the place where, in 1914, Raggedy Ann was created.
- was first explored in 1673 by the French explorer Robert Cavelier, sieur de La Salle.

Read the clues and unscramble the words about Indiana.

Lincoln's first name __ __ __ __ ◯ __ ◯ M A B A R A H

A car made in South Bend __ __ ◯ __ ◯ __ __ __ ◯ __ K R A T U S E B D E

Indianapolis's football team ◯ __ __ ◯◯ __ S L O C T

Unscramble the circled letters to find the name of the American Indian chief who was defeated at the Battle of Tippecanoe.

__ __ __ __ __ __ __ __

Famous Indianans

- William Henry Harrison, whose home was in Indianapolis, was the ninth president.
- Virgil Grissom was an astronaut and has an air force base named after him.
- Kurt Vonnegut Jr. was a famous science-fiction writer.
- J. Danforth Quayle served as vice president during the term of President George H. W. Bush.
- James Whitcomb Riley was a poet who wrote "When the Frost Is on the Punkin."
- David Letterman hosts a late-night talk show.
- Abraham Lincoln worked on a family farm in Indiana as a boy.

State Greats

- The Indianapolis Motor Speedway hosts the Indianapolis 500 and the Brickyard 400.
- The Indianapolis Children's Museum is the largest in the world.
- The first professional baseball game was played in Fort Wayne in 1871.
- Santa Claus, Indiana, receives over 500,000 letters and requests at Christmastime.
- Indiana is home to both the Indiana Pacers and the Indianapolis Colts.
- The Studebaker automobile was built in South Bend.

Most Ears of Corn on a Single Plant
October 13, 2009

If you have ever picked corn, you probably know that one plant usually produces only a couple of ears. And, of those ears, usually only one is big enough eat. In 2009, however, Tyler Craig managed to grow a record-setting corn plant in Swedesburg, Iowa. The single plant grew 16 ears of corn! Tyler's grandfather is a crop farmer who gave Tyler the seed that grew into the award-winning corn plant. Tyler planted the seed in an unlikely place—his mother's lily garden.

A painting by Iowa artist Grant Wood inspired the design of the Iowa quarter. The scene on the quarter shows people planting a tree beside a schoolhouse.

State Facts

Iowa
Des Moines ★

Statehood: 12/28/1846
Rank: 29
Nicknames: Hawkeye State, Corn State
Population: 3,046,355 (2010)
State Flower: Wild rose
State Bird: Eastern goldfinch
State Tree: Oak
State Song: "Song of Iowa"
Motto: *Our Liberties We Prize, and Our Rights We Will Maintain*
Postal Code: IA

Fun Facts (2009)
Amusement Parks: 4
Toy Stores: 99
Pet and Pet Supply Stores: 75

Did You Know?

Iowa
- is called "the Land Where the Corn Grows Tall."
- is mostly flat and was once covered by glaciers.
- is the nation's leading producer of hogs and corn.
- is bordered on the east by the Mississippi River and on the west by the Missouri River.
- is the birthplace of Herbert Hoover, the thirty-first president.

Read the clues. Unscramble the words about Iowa.

This is produced in Sioux City. __ ◯ __ __ __ ◯ __   R P O C P O N

He invented the electric razor. ◯ __ __ ◯ __ __ __   K S C C H I

He'll wash your clothes. ◯ __ __ __ __ __   Y A M A T G

Lead was mined in this city. ◯ __ __ __ __ ◯ __   Q U E B U D U

The famed birthplace of Kirk __ __ __ __ ◯ __ __ ◯   S R I V E I D E R

Unscramble the circled letters to find Iowa's capital.

__ __ __ __ __ __ __ __ __ __

Famous Iowans

- Bob Feller is a Hall of Fame pitcher who played for the Cleveland Indians.
- Fred Maytag sold washing machines.
- John Wayne won an Academy Award for his movie, *True Grit*, but was most famous for his many Westerns.
- Jacob Schick grew up in Des Moines and invented the electric razor.
- Herbert Hoover served as the thirty-first president of the United States.
- Glenn Miller led the famous Glenn Miller Orchestra.

State Greats

- More than 90 percent of Iowa's land is farmland.
- More than 50 insurance companies have their headquarters in Des Moines.
- In 1890, William Morrison built the first electric car in the United States. It traveled at 20 miles per hour.
- The *Star Trek* character Captain James T. Kirk was said to have been born in Iowa. The town of Riverside holds a birthday party for him every year.

First Woman to Play with the Harlem Globetrotters
1985

Olympic basketball player Lynette Woodard was the First Woman to Play with the Harlem Globetrotters. The Globetrotters combine fantastic basketball with hilarious entertainment. Dribbles and dunks are part of their game, but so are clowns and comedians. Woodard played with the team for two years. Born in Wichita, Kansas, Woodard was a standout at the University of Kansas. She was also captain of the 1984 US Olympic gold medal–winning basketball team and became a member of the Women's Basketball Hall of Fame.

The Kansas quarter features images of a buffalo and a sunflower, which were abundant throughout the state when it earned its statehood in 1861.

State Facts

Kansas

Topeka ★

Statehood: 1/29/1861
Rank: 34
Nickname: Sunflower State
Population: 2,853,118 (2010)
State Flower: Common sunflower
State Bird: Western meadowlark
State Tree: Eastern cottonwood
State Song: "Home on the Range"
Motto: *To the Stars Through Difficulties*
Postal Code: KS

Fun Facts (2009)
Amusement Parks: 2
Toy Stores: 80
Pet and Pet Supply Stores: 78

Did You Know?

KANSAS

Kansas
- is often called the "breadbasket of America."
- lies in the geographic center of North America.
- traditionally leads the nation in wheat production.
- is the childhood home of Dwight D. Eisenhower, the thirty-fourth president.
- was part of the "Dust Bowl" during the Great Depression of the 1930s.

The motto of Kansas is: *Ad astra per aspera*.

Unscramble the letters below to find what the motto means.

"

O T   H E T   S R A S T   G H R O U H T

__ ___ _____ _____

F I C I D U T F I L E S

_____."

Rewrite the motto in your own words. What do you think it means?

_____

_____

Think of a personal motto for yourself. Write it below.

_____

Famous Kansans

- Melissa Etheridge, a popular singer, was born in Leavenworth.
- Amelia Earhart was the first woman to fly across the Atlantic Ocean. She was born in Atchison.
- "Wild Bill" Hickok was a scout and frontier marshal in the Old West.
- Bob Dole was a US senator for many years.
- Charlie "Bird" Parker was born in the 1920s. He is one of the greatest jazz musicians in American history.
- Wilt Chamberlain played on the basketball team of the University of Kansas located in Lawrence.

State Greats

- The first American salt was produced in Hutchinson in 1888.
- The Kansas railroads in Abilene and Dodge City made it possible to ship cattle and agricultural products to the east.
- The Dwight D. Eisenhower Museum and Library is located in Abilene.
- Factories in Wichita lead the nation in the production of small aircraft.
- Kansas is in the center of the original 48 states.
- Lawrence was a key point in the Underground Railroad to help slaves escape from the South.

Smallest Living Dog by Height
May 12, 2007

Do good things really come in small packages? Lana Elswick would know. Her dog Boo Boo holds the record for the Smallest Living Dog by Height. Little Boo Boo is a female long-haired Chihuahua who lives with Elswick in Raceland, Kentucky. Chihuahuas normally range from 6 to 8 inches tall and weigh about 2 to 6 pounds. But, this record-setting dog is only 4 inches tall. That's only a little taller than a coffee mug. Boo Boo weighs 1.5 pounds. She was born on April 15, 2006.

The Kentucky quarter features a horse in front of the mansion where Stephen Foster wrote the state song "My Old Kentucky Home." The horse symbolizes the Kentucky Derby.

State Facts

Kentucky
★ Frankfort

Statehood: 6/1/1792
Rank: 15
Nickname: Bluegrass State
Population: 4,339,367 (2010)
State Flower: Goldenrod
State Bird: Cardinal
State Tree: Tulip poplar
State Song: "My Old Kentucky Home"
Motto: *United We Stand, Divided We Fall*
Postal Code: KY

Fun Facts (2009)
Amusement Parks: 9
Toy Stores: 70
Pet and Pet Supply Stores: 64

Did You Know?

Kentucky
- is the location of the United States Gold Depository at Fort Knox.
- is the location of the Cumberland Gap, an important passageway for early explorers.
- is the nation's leading producer of bituminous coal.
- sided with the Union during the Civil War, even though it is a southern state.
- is the birthplace of Abraham Lincoln, the sixteenth president, and Jefferson Davis, president of the Confederate States of America during the Civil War.

Answer the questions to learn the Kentucky state motto.

Who was the sixteenth president? ___ ___ ___ ___ ___ ___
  1   5

What famous explorer settled in Kentucky? ___ ___ ___ ___ ___ ___ ___ ___ ___ ___
  3   6   4   2

What Kentucky city is on the Ohio River? ___ ___ ___ ___ ___ ___ ___ ___ ___ ___
  7   8   9

In what city are Corvettes made? ___ ___ ___ ___ ___ ___ ___ ___ ___
  10

What is the capital of Kentucky? ___ ___ ___ ___ ___ ___ ___ ___ ___
  11   12

Kentucky state motto:

" ___ ___ ___ ___ ___ ___   ___ ___   ___ ___ ___ ___ ___ ,
  7   4   5   12 2   3   10 2   8   12 6   4   3

___ ___ ___ ___ ___ ___ ___   ___ ___   ___ ___ ___ ___ ."
  3   5   9   5   3   2   3   10 2   11 6   1   1

Famous Kentuckians

- Abraham Lincoln was born in Kentucky.
- Jefferson Davis was the president of the Confederacy.
- Carry Nation was the leader of the temperance movement.
- Muhammad Ali was a boxer.
- Diane Sawyer is a broadcast journalist.
- Rosemary Clooney was a singer and an actress who appeared in the movie *White Christmas*.
- Loretta Lynn is a country and western singer.

State Greats

- All Chevrolet Corvettes are made in Bowling Green.
- The Kentucky Derby, run at Churchill Downs in Louisville, is the oldest continuously held horse race.
- The first Kentucky Fried Chicken owned and operated by Colonel Sanders is in Corbin.
- Heather Renee French Henry was crowned Miss America in 2000.
- Mammoth Cave National Park is the world's longest cave.
- Fort Knox, where America's gold is stored, is an actual modern-day fort.

Louisiana

Largest Jambalaya
May 23, 2009

Most people in Louisiana would probably say that jambalaya is a simple one-pot meal to prepare. But, how simple is preparing 3,371 pounds of the spicy Louisiana dish? The Jambalaya Festival Association in Gonzales, Louisiana, made the world's Largest Jambalaya. The dish contained pork, sausages, rice, onions, salt, black pepper, red pepper, garlic, water, and oil. The rice alone weighed 650 pounds, not to mention the other ingredients. It's no wonder that the cooks needed a pot that was 7 feet 8 inches high.

The Louisiana quarter features an image of a trumpet to celebrate the birth of jazz music there. It also includes an image of the state bird and an outline of the Louisiana Purchase.

State Facts

Louisiana

Baton Rouge

Statehood: 4/30/1812
Rank: 18
Nickname: Pelican State
Population: 4,533,372 (2010)
State Flower: Magnolia flower
State Bird: Eastern brown pelican
State Tree: Bald cypress
State Song: "Give Me Louisiana," "You Are My Sunshine"
Motto: *Union, Justice, Confidence*
Postal Code: LA

Fun Facts (2009)
Amusement Parks: 4
Toy Stores: 88
Pet and Pet Supply Stores: 85

Did You Know?

Louisiana
- accounts for almost 90 percent of all crayfish produced in the world.
- was once claimed for France by the French explorer Robert Cavelier, sieur de La Salle.
- was part of the Louisiana Purchase, a huge land parcel purchased from Napoleon of France in 1803.
- is important to everyone who loves jazz music, Cajun and Creole cooking, and Mardi Gras.
- has New Orleans, a city built where the Mississippi River empties into the Gulf of Mexico.

Find and circle the seven words about Louisiana hidden in the word search below. Then, fill in the sentences below with the words found in the word search.

R	E	S	C	A	R	T	E	C	A	D	D	O	C
M	L	J	S	A	T	C	H	M	O	G	A	M	A
M	A	C	C	K	N	O	T	H	J	Y	O	U	P
P	B	R	L	A	S	A	L	L	E	I	N	S	O
C	E	F	C	H	J	B	A	Y	E	O	X	O	T
S	A	L	A	C	L	U	W	P	O	U	N	C	E
C	H	R	I	M	A	G	N	O	L	I	A	E	X
T	A	L	R	C	U	R	T	G	O	Y	S	D	P
Y	E	L	E	J	A	M	A	R	Z	B	H	Y	E
P	J	F	D	N	B	N	P	S	A	L	E	Z	L

_____ was the nickname given to the jazz legend from New Orleans.

_____, the playwright and author, was born in New Orleans.

The _____ is the state flower of Louisiana.

_____ music was created in southwest Louisiana.

The _____ earned Louisiana its nickname.

The _____ American Indians were among the first peoples of Louisiana.

The French explorer _____ named Louisiana after King Louis XIV.

Famous Louisianans

- Pinckney Pinchback was the country's first African American state governor.
- New Orleans was the birthplace of famous American author and playwright Truman Capote.
- Gospel legend Mahalia Jackson was born in New Orleans.
- Football player and Fox TV Sports announcer Terry Bradshaw was born in Shreveport.
- Jazz legend Louis Armstrong, also called "Satchmo," was born and raised in New Orleans.
- Jerry Lee Lewis, one of the first rock-and-roll stars, is from Ferriday.

State Greats

- Zydeco, a mix of French and blues music, began in southwest Louisiana.
- The McIlhenny family on Avery "Island" invented Tabasco sauce.
- The Second Lake Pontchartrain Causeway is the longest bridge of its type in the world.
- The Mardi Gras Festival in New Orleans is one of the country's most famous festivals.
- The tallest state capitol building in the United States is in Baton Rouge. The building is 34 stories high.
- The Mississippi, the longest river in the United States, meets the ocean in New Orleans.

Maine

Tallest Snowman
February 26, 2008

The Tallest Snowman in the world is not a snowman at all, but a snow woman! In 2008, residents of Bethel, Maine, built the record-breaking snow woman. Volunteers pitched in throughout the month of February to build the 13-million-pound snow woman. Volunteers used spruce trees for her arms, and they used tires to make her bright red lips and buttons. Middle school students sewed her a red fleece hat. The final result was "Olympia," a 122-foot-tall snow woman!

The Maine quarter shows an image of the Pemaquid Point lighthouse, which was built six years after Maine became a state. The ship represents the importance of shipping in the state.

State Facts

Maine

Augusta ★

Statehood: 3/15/1820
Rank: 23
Nickname: Pine Tree State
Population: 1,328,361 (2010)
State Flower: White pine cone and tassel
State Bird: Chickadee
State Tree: White pine
State Song: "State of Maine Song"
Motto: *I Lead*
Postal Code: ME

Fun Facts (2009)
Amusement Parks: 3
Toy Stores: 43
Pet and Pet Supply Stores: 51

Did You Know?

Maine
- is known as "Down East."
- once belonged to Massachusetts.
- is bordered on the north by Canada.
- is famous for its lobsters.
- was probably visited by the first European when Leif Ericson, a Viking leader, arrived around AD 1000.
- is the home state of Margaret Chase Smith, the first woman to have been elected to both houses of the US Congress.

Read the clues. Unscramble the words about Maine.

Stephen King's home   ⃝ __ __ __ ⃝ __   O N B R A G

capital city of Maine   __ __ __ __ ⃝ __ __   U S A G U A T

St. Vincent Millay's prize   __ __ __ __ ⃝ __ ⃝   Z R P I E L T U

nickname tree   __ __ __ ⃝   E P N I

Lincoln's vice president   __ __ __ ⃝ __ __   A N H I L M

Unscramble the circled letters to find Maine's main export.

__ __ __ __ __ __ __

Famous Mainers

- Henry Wadsworth Longfellow wrote the poem "Paul Revere's Ride."
- Hannibal Hamlin was Abraham Lincoln's vice president.
- Edna St. Vincent Millay won the Pulitzer Prize for poetry.
- Edmund Muskie was an important senator.
- Stephen King lives in Bangor and writes horror novels.
- Leon Leonwood "L.L." Bean started the L.L. Bean company in Freeport.
- Harriet Beecher Stowe published over 30 books, but is best known for her best-selling antislavery novel *Uncle Tom's Cabin*.

State Greats

- Maine is the only state to share a border with only one other state—New Hampshire. Canada forms the other land borders.
- The first naval battle of the Revolutionary War took place near Machias.
- Nearly 90 percent of all lobster caught in the United States is caught off the coast of Maine. Many fishermen dock their boats in Rockland.
- Maine's nickname is the "Pine Tree State." Almost 90 percent of the state is covered by forests.

Longest Nose Wheelie on a Motocross Bike
August 22, 2010

It's not easy to ride a bike on one wheel, especially when the back wheel is way up in the air. This is called a nose wheelie, and it's quite a stunt. Gary Harding performed the longest nose wheelie of all time on a Kawasaki KX250T8F bike. He kept his bike's nose to the road for 282 feet 10 inches at the Mason-Dixon Dragway in Boonsboro, Maryland. After happily setting the record, Harding immediately proposed marriage to his girlfriend on the track. Her answer was yes.

The Maryland quarter features an image of the dome of the Maryland State House building in Annapolis. It is the oldest state capitol building still in regular use by its legislature.

State Facts

Maryland

Annapolis

Statehood: 4/28/1788
Rank: 7
Nicknames: Old Line State, Free State
Population: 5,773,552 (2010)
State Flower: Black-eyed Susan
State Bird: Baltimore oriole
State Tree: White oak
State Song: "Maryland, My Maryland"
Motto: *Strong Deeds, Gentle Words*
Postal Code: MD

Fun Facts (2009)
Amusement Parks: 8
Toy Stores: 144
Pet and Pet Supply Stores: 159

Did You Know?

Maryland
- was named for Queen Henrietta Maria, the wife of Charles I of England.
- is almost cut in half by the Chesapeake Bay.
- was explored in 1608 by Captain John Smith.
- is the home of the United States Naval Academy at Annapolis.
- is where Francis Scott Key wrote "The Star-Spangled Banner" while watching the British bombard Fort McHenry at Baltimore.

Write the letter from column B next to the matching phrase in column A.

1. _____ from here to the Navy

2. _____ passes by Washington, DC

3. _____ has a large natural harbor

4. _____ cuts through Maryland

5. _____ across the Potomac from Maryland

6. _____ east of Maryland

(A) Delaware

(B) Potomac River

(C) Annapolis

(D) Chesapeake Bay

(E) Virginia

(F) Baltimore

Famous Marylanders

- Frederick Douglass, born a slave, escaped from his master. He started a newspaper called *North Star*.
- John Wilkes Booth was an actor and the man who assassinated Abraham Lincoln.
- Babe Ruth was perhaps the greatest baseball player ever.
- Harriet Tubman escaped from slavery and helped free more than 300 slaves through the Underground Railroad.
- Thurgood Marshall was the first African American Supreme Court justice.
- Billie Holiday was a popular jazz singer in the 1930s.

State Greats

- In 1784, the very first hot air balloon lifted off from Maryland.
- The Baltimore and Ohio Railroad Company built the first passenger train in the United States.
- Maryland's northern border is the Mason-Dixon line, which was drawn to separate the North from the South during the Civil War.
- Francis Scott Key, a lawyer from Maryland, saw a War of 1812 battle at Fort McHenry and wrote "The Star-Spangled Banner."
- The US Naval Academy, in Annapolis, trains students to become officers in the Navy.

Largest Ice Cream Cup
September 13, 2005

Anniversaries are special days. Sometimes, people celebrate them in unusual ways. In 2005, an ice cream company had its 60th anniversary. To celebrate, the company tried to break a world record in Canton, Massachusetts, by making the world's Largest Ice Cream Cup. Breaking the record was not easy though. First, the participants had to make the giant cup. Then, six people scooped 1,289 gallons of vanilla ice cream into the cup for 15 hours. When they were done, the record-breaking ice cream cup weighed 8,865 pounds or about the weight of three cars.

Two children designed the Massachusetts quarter. Featured in front of the state is an image of the famous Minuteman statue.

State Facts

Massachusetts
Boston

Statehood: 2/6/1788
Rank: 6
Nicknames: Bay State, Old Colony State
Population: 6,547,629 (2010)
State Flower: Mayflower
State Bird: Black-capped chickadee
State Tree: American elm
State Song: "All Hail to Massachusetts"
Motto: *By the Sword We Seek Peace, but Peace Only Under Liberty*
Postal Code: MA

Fun Facts (2009)
Amusement Parks: 5
Toy Stores: 207
Pet and Pet Supply Stores: 174

Did You Know?

Massachusetts
- is the location of Salem, the site of the infamous witchcraft trials of 1692.
- is the location of Plymouth, the place where the Pilgrims landed in 1620.
- is the birthplace of John F. Kennedy, the thirty-fifth president, who was a senator from this state.
- is where, in April of 1775, the Revolutionary War began when patriots fought the British at Lexington and Concord.

Write the letter from column B next to the matching phrase in column A.

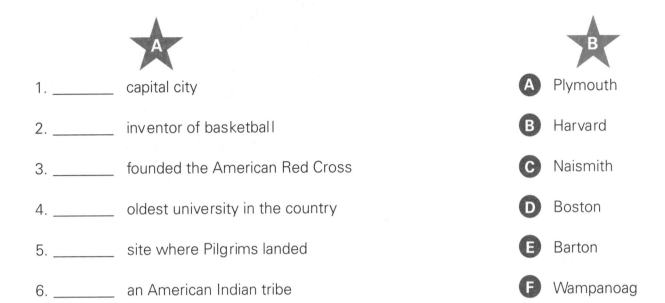

A

1. _____ capital city

2. _____ inventor of basketball

3. _____ founded the American Red Cross

4. _____ oldest university in the country

5. _____ site where Pilgrims landed

6. _____ an American Indian tribe

B

A Plymouth

B Harvard

C Naismith

D Boston

E Barton

F Wampanoag

Famous Bay Staters

- John Adams and John Quincy Adams were presidents.
- Paul Revere rode from Charlestown to Lexington on April 18, 1775, warning patriots of the arrival of British troops.
- Clara Barton founded the American Red Cross.
- Emily Dickinson wrote poetry in her Amherst home.
- Ralph Waldo Emerson was a poet and an essayist.
- Bette Davis starred in films throughout the 1930s, '40s, and '50s.
- Barbara Walters is a well-known television commentator.

State Greats

- Harvard University in Cambridge is the oldest college in the country.
- Francis Cabot Lowell opened several manufacturing mills in the early 1800s. The town of East Chelmsford was renamed Lowell in his honor.
- In 1891, James Naismith invented the game of basketball in Springfield.
- Boston, Massachusetts' capital, is home to Boston Harbor—the site of the Boston Tea Party where colonists dumped tea into the water to protest the tax on tea.
- Cape Cod and the islands off the coast of Massachusetts are popular vacation spots.

Largest Hamburger Commercially Available
January 26, 2011

Many restaurants serve hamburgers in different sizes. They serve double burgers and triple burgers. Sometimes they sell burgers by their weight. But, no burger even comes close to the one offered at a restaurant in Southgate, Michigan. The burger weighs 319 pounds and costs $1,800. It's easy to understand why it takes more than one person to lift it. And, yes, it comes on a bun with pickles, cheese, bacon, lettuce, tomatoes, and onions!

The Michigan quarter features the state's outline and the Great Lakes: Huron, Ontario, Michigan, Erie, and Superior. The lakes are an important part of the state's history and economy.

State Facts

Statehood: 1/26/1837
Rank: 26
Nickname: Great Lakes State
Population: 9,883,640 (2010)
State Flower: Apple blossom
State Bird: American robin
State Tree: White pine
State Song: "Michigan, My Michigan"
Motto: *If You Seek a Pleasant Peninsula, Look About You*
Postal Code: MI

Fun Facts (2009)
Amusement Parks: 10
Toy Stores: 295
Pet and Pet Supply Stores: 302

Did You Know?

Michigan
- has another nickname—the "Wolverine State."
- shares a border with Canada.
- is home to Greenfield Village, where visitors can see Henry Ford's birthplace and Thomas Edison's laboratory.
- once fought with Ohio over the land around what is now the city of Toledo, Ohio.
- has two separate sections—the Upper Peninsula and the Lower Peninsula.

Read the clues. Unscramble the words about Michigan.

★ President Ford's first name D A R G L E _ _ _ _ _ _

★ lightbulb man S I D O N E _ _ _ _ _ _

★ Chief N O P I A C T _ _ _ _ _ _ _

★ automotive center R O I T T E D _ _ _ _ _ _ _

★ Commodore Perry's place K A L E I E R _ _ _ _ _ _ _ _ _

★ Unscramble the circled letters to find Michigan's capital.

_ _ _ _ _ _ _

Famous Michiganders

- Ralph Bunche was the first African American to win the Nobel Peace Prize.
- Harriet Quimby was the first licensed American female pilot.
- Chief Pontiac was leader of the Ottawa.
- Henry Ford created the modern automobile industry.
- Gerald Ford became thirty-eighth president of the United States.
- Della Reese is an actress and a singer.
- Edna Ferber is a novelist.

State Greats

- Michigan is the only state made up of two peninsulas. They are called the Upper Peninsula and the Lower Peninsula.
- Corn flakes cereal was invented at Battle Creek.
- More cars and trucks are made in Michigan than any other state. The city of Detroit is the center of the automobile industry.
- The Henry Ford Museum and Greenfield Village are in Dearborn. Thomas Edison's laboratory where he invented the lightbulb was moved here from New Jersey. It also features some of the first cars made by Henry Ford.

Most People Static Cycling
March 7, 2010

Turn on the music and spin those wheels! A whole lot of people got on a whole lot of static (or *stationary*) bikes in a sports arena in Minneapolis, Minnesota, to break a world record. The Most People Static Cycling together is 1,052. The participants set the record at "Ride of a Lifetime," an event held by a fitness club organization. The organization brought in 1,063 bikes for the event. That's a whole lot of spinning wheels!

The Minnesota quarter features the state's outline, along with a typical Minnesota lake scene that shows a canoe with people fishing, pine trees, and Minnesota's state bird, the loon.

State Facts

Statehood: 5/11/1858
Rank: 32
Nicknames: North Star State, Gopher State, Bread and Butter State
Population: 5,303,925 (2010)
State Flower: Pink and white lady slipper
State Bird: Common loon
State Tree: Red pine
State Song: "Hail! Minnesota"
Motto: *Star of the North*
Postal Code: MN

Fun Facts (2009)
Amusement Parks: 9
Toy Stores: 179
Pet and Pet Supply Stores: 147

Did You Know?

Minnesota
- is known as the "Land of 10,000 Lakes."
- is the location of the northernmost point in the continental United States.
- is said to have been the home of fabled lumberjack Paul Bunyan.
- is the location of Duluth, the busiest freshwater port in North America.
- boasts the Mall of America, the largest shopping mall in the United States.

Read the clues. Unscramble the words about Minnesota.

Lake __ __ __ __ __ __ __ __   P S U E O I R R

Vice President Humphrey's first name __ __ __ __ __ __   R E H B T U

Fort __ __ __ __ __ __ __ __   N L E G S I N L

Lindbergh flew
nonstop across this ocean __ __ __ __ __ __ __ __   T T L A A I C N

Minnesota's capital __ __ __ __ __ __ __   P U A T S L

Minnesota's American Indians __ __ __ __ __ __   A J O B I W

Famous Minnesotans

- Charles Lindbergh was the first aviator to fly solo, nonstop, across the Atlantic Ocean.
- Charles Bender, an Ojibwa baseball pitcher, was elected to the Baseball Hall of Fame in 1951.
- Judy Garland, an actress who played Dorothy in *The Wizard of Oz*, was born in Grand Rapids.
- Hubert H. Humphrey became vice president of the United States.
- Charles Schulz created the *Peanuts* comic strip.
- Bob Dylan, singer and songwriter, was born in Duluth.

State Greats

- Minnesota has the northernmost point of the continental United States.
- Minnesota's capital, St. Paul, is part of a Twin City system with Minneapolis.
- The Port of Duluth-Superior is the busiest port on the Great Lakes.
- Fort Snelling was built at the fork of the Mississippi and Minnesota rivers in the 1820s.
- The Mayo Clinic is in Rochester and is famous throughout the world.

Most Hair Donated to Charity in 24 Hours
May 21, 2007

People find many ways to help others. Some people give money. Others run races or ride bikes to raise money. In 2007, hundreds of people in Clinton, Mississippi, donated their hair for charity. They wanted to help women who had lost their hair because of medical treatment for illness. The Most Hair Donated to Charity in 24 Hours is 107.4 pounds. A total of 881 people donated their hair at the Mississippi Institute for Aesthetics, Nails, and Cosmetology.

The Mississippi quarter features the state tree and flower, the magnolia. In 1900, schoolchildren chose the magnolia as the state flower. Other children chose the state tree in 1935.

State Facts

Mississippi
★ Jackson

Statehood: 12/10/1817
Rank: 20
Nickname: Magnolia State
Population: 2,967,297 (2010)
State Flower: Magnolia flower
State Bird: Mockingbird
State Tree: Magnolia
State Song: "Go Mississippi"
Motto: *By Valor and Arms*
Postal Code: MS

Fun Facts (2009)
Amusement Parks: 4
Toy Stores: 32
Pet and Pet Supply Stores: 30

Did You Know?

Mississippi
- is where Coca-Cola was first bottled.
- is the birthplace of Elvis Presley, one of the most popular singers of the 1900s.
- is the ancestral home of the Chickasaw and the Natchez, two American Indian nations.
- became the second state to leave the Union at the start of the Civil War in 1861.

Next to each sentence write a *T* if the statement is true or an *F* if the statement is false.

_____ Mississippi is bordered by five states.

_____ The Mississippi River drains into the Pacific Ocean.

_____ The fishing industry helped rebuild the state.

_____ Coca-Cola was invented in Mississippi.

_____ The Natchez tribe fought against the French settlers.

_____ Biloxi has always been Mississippi's capital.

_____ The "Trail of Tears" refers to the march many American Indians were forced to take.

Famous Mississippians

- Charles and Medgar Evers were civil rights leaders.
- Author William Faulkner won a Nobel Prize and two Pulitzer Prizes.
- Oprah Winfrey has her own TV network and starred in *The Color Purple.*
- Richard Wright wrote stories of his youth in the South.
- Walter Payton was a football player for the Chicago Bears.
- John Lee Hooker is one of the greatest blues singers and guitarists.
- Elvis Presley became one of the most loved musicians in the world.

State Greats

- A lot of the upholstered, or padded, furniture in stores comes from Mississippi.
- Every April, people from all over the world come to Belzoni to attend the World Catfish Festival.
- Coca-Cola, invented in Georgia, was first bottled in Vicksburg, Mississippi.
- The Tennessee-Tombigbee Waterway was built to connect two rivers and make transportation easier.
- The Mississippi River is the longest river system in North America and the third longest in the world.

Missouri

Tallest Commemorative Monument
October 28, 1965

Monuments are built to help us remember events or people who have done something important. The Gateway Arch in Saint Louis, Missouri, was built to honor the frontier families who traveled from Saint Louis to explore the western part of the United States. The sweeping arch spans 630 feet and rises to the same height. Construction began in February 1963 and was completed in October 1965. The Arch, which cost $13 million to build, weighs 17,246 tons.

The Missouri quarter joins images relating to two major events in the state's history. In 1804, Lewis and Clark explored the Missouri River. In 1965, the famous Gateway Arch was built.

State Facts

Statehood: 8/10/1821
Rank: 24
Nickname: Show Me State
Population: 5,988,927 (2010)
State Flower: White hawthorn blossom
State Bird: Bluebird
State Tree: Flowering dogwood
State Song: "Missouri Waltz"
Motto: *Let the Welfare of the People Be the Supreme Law*
Postal Code: MO

Fun Facts (2009)
Amusement Parks: 11
Toy Stores: 180
Pet and Pet Supply Stores: 159

Did You Know?

Missouri
- is the location of the famous Gateway Arch.
- is the place where Mark Twain, creator of Tom Sawyer and Huckleberry Finn, lived.
- is the home state of Harry S. Truman, the thirty-third president.
- was the starting point for Lewis and Clark's 1804 Journey of Discovery.
- was the eastern destination of the Pony Express, which connected the eastern United States with California.

Read the clues. Unscramble the words about Missouri.

a famous guide __ __ __ __ __ __   R O N S A C

a president of the United States __ __ __ __ __ __   M U N R A T

one of America's greatest scientists __ __ __ __ __ __   R E V A R C

Mark Twain's boyhood home __ __ __ __ __ __ __ __   N A H I N L A B

admitted as a free state
by the Missouri Compromise __ __ __ __ __   N E M I A

a large dam __ __ __ __ __ __ __ __   G L B N E A L

Famous Missourians

- Harry S. Truman was president of the United States. His home and library are located in Independence.
- Christopher Carson, later known as Kit Carson, grew up in Missouri and became a famous guide.
- Samuel Clemens, known as Mark Twain, had his boyhood home in Hannibal.
- George Washington Carver became one of America's greatest scientists.
- Daniel Boone moved to Missouri in 1799 and lived the last 20 years of his life there.
- Langston Hughes was one of America's most famous African American poets.

State Greats

- Bagnell Dam across from the Osage River in the Ozarks is one of the largest man-made lakes in the world. It covers 65,000 acres.
- In 1860, the Pony Express was started at St. Joseph, Missouri.
- Jefferson City, a small riverboat town, was chosen as the capital in 1821. The town was laid out by Daniel M. Boone, son of the famous Daniel Boone.
- Missouri is the home of the St. Louis Rams and the Kansas City Chiefs football teams.

Montana

Largest Snowflake
January 28, 1887

A snowflake is made up of tiny crystals, each with six sides. A snowflake's size depends on how many crystals stick together. Most snowflakes easily fit on a fingertip. During a wet snowfall, snowflakes can become fairly large. But, have you ever seen or heard of a snowflake as large as a computer screen? In January 1887, ranch owner Matt Coleman measured a huge snowflake in Fort Keogh, Montana. It was a whopping 15 inches wide and 8 inches thick.

The Montana quarter features an image of a bison skull above Montana's diverse landscape. The bison skull symbolizes the American Indian tribes that once lived in the area.

State Facts

Montana
Helena

Statehood: 11/8/1889
Rank: 41
Nickname: Treasure State
Population: 989,415 (2010)
State Flower: Bitterroot
State Bird: Western meadowlark
State Tree: Ponderosa pine
State Song: "Montana"
Motto: *Gold and Silver*
Postal Code: MT

Fun Facts (2009)
Amusement Parks: 5
Toy Stores: 48
Pet and Pet Supply Stores: 24

Did You Know?

Montana
- is the location of Glacier National Park.
- is the home of Pompey's Pillar, a famous landmark used by pioneers in their migration to the West.
- is where, at the Battle of Little Bighorn in 1876, Custer's Last Stand was fought.
- is where, in 1842, Jesuit missionaries established St. Mary's mission, the first attempt at a permanent settlement in the state.

Read the clues. Circle each hidden word and draw a line to the phrase it answers.

the metal that started a "rush" to the area   U S T E V E N S V I L L E A

drawings found in caves   Y U R E Y O

last name of famous chemist   F F G O L D B

the first town   L P I C T O G R A P H S B

an animal hunted by Crow and Blackfeet American Indians   F F B U F F A L O X

Famous Montanans

- Robert Yellowtail was the first American Indian hired by the US government to lead a reservation.
- Plenty Coups was a Crow leader who represented the American Indian nations at a ceremony for the Tomb of the Unknown Soldier.
- Lester Carl Thurow, born in Livingston, was an economist and an author.
- Harold Clayton Urey grew up in Montana and won the Nobel Prize for chemistry.
- Politician Jeannette Rankin was from Missoula. She was the only person to vote against both World Wars.

State Greats

- Fort Peck Dam is one of the biggest dams in the world.
- In 1876, Lieutenant Colonel George Armstrong Custer was defeated at the famous Battle of Little Bighorn.
- Visitors can see snow year-round at Glacier National Park.
- Pictograph Cave State Historic Site near Billings has cave drawings that are more than 5,000 years old.
- Giant Springs is one of the largest fresh water springs—338 million gallons of water flow through it each day.

Widest Tornado Damage Path
May 22, 2004

A tornado is a funnel-shaped cloud of whirling wind that can cause a lot of damage. One day in May 2004, 56 tornadoes occurred in the Midwest. One of them, known as the Hallam Nebraska tornado, left a wide path of destruction. The Widest Tornado Damage Path was estimated at 2.49 miles wide. Wind speeds were as high as 100 miles per hour. The tornado toppled train cars off a freight train, uprooted sturdy trees, and destroyed many well-built homes and farms.

The Nebraska state quarter features a pioneer family traveling westward in a covered wagon. Behind them is the 480-foot Chimney Rock, rising from the valley of the North Platte River.

State Facts

Statehood: 3/1/1867
Rank: 37
Nickname: Cornhusker State
Population: 1,826,341 (2010)
State Flower: Goldenrod
State Bird: Western meadowlark
State Tree: Cottonwood
State Song: "Beautiful Nebraska"
Motto: *Equality Before the Law*
Postal Code: NE

Fun Facts (2009)
Amusement Parks: 1
Toy Stores: 72
Pet and Pet Supply Stores: 44

Did You Know?

Nebraska
- is the location of Chimney Rock in the North Platte River Valley, an important landmark for early pioneers traveling along the Oregon Trail.
- has a greater percentage of farmland than any other state.
- is the birthplace of Gerald Ford, the thirty-eighth president.
- once contained the Dakota and Colorado territories.

Next to each sentence write a _T_ if the statement is true or an _F_ if the statement is false.

_____ The Till Plains are more fertile than the Great Plains.

_____ Omaha is closer to Colorado than it is to Iowa.

_____ The city of Lincoln is in the Till Plains.

_____ The first frozen dinners were made in Lincoln.

_____ There are few trees in Nebraska.

_____ Now, most people in Nebraska live in cities.

_____ To get into Iowa, northern Nebraskans would have to cross the Platte River.

Famous Nebraskans

- Malcolm Little was born in Omaha. He changed his name to Malcolm X and became a civil rights leader.
- Actor Henry Fonda is the father of actors Jane Fonda and Peter Fonda and grandfather of actor Bridget Fonda.
- Fred Astaire was a dancer who appeared in more than 30 film musicals.
- Crazy Horse was an American Indian who fought against US settlers to reclaim land for his people.
- Bob Gibson twice won the Cy Young award, baseball's top award for pitchers.

State Greats

- Nebraska held the world's first rodeo in 1882. It starred Buffalo Bill Cody.
- The first fossil of a woolly mammoth was found in Nebraska. It is more than 13 feet high.
- The largest planted forest in the country is the Nebraska National Forest. It covers 22,000 acres.
- Millions of buffalo used to roam through Nebraska. They were hunted nearly to extinction but are now protected.
- The first frozen dinners came from Omaha, Nebraska.
- Despite the Nebraska National Forest, only 2 percent of the state is forest.

Nevada

Largest Fuzzy Dice
November 11, 2011

Dice are among the oldest game pieces. They were first used for playing games thousands of years ago. Back then, dice were made of bone, ivory, bronze, marble, or other kinds of rock. In 2011, the Las Vegas Convention and Visitors Authority unveiled a huge pair of bright orange and pink dice in Las Vegas, Nevada. Not only were they loudly colored and fuzzy, but they were the Largest Fuzzy Dice ever. Each measured 4 feet by 4 feet by 4 feet. Organizers presented the dice at a "lucky" time too—11:11 am eastern standard time.

The Nevada quarter features an image of wild mustangs framed by clusters of sagebrush flowers. More than half of America's wild horses live in Nevada.

State Facts

Statehood: 10/31/1864
Rank: 36
Nicknames: The Silver State, Sagebrush State, Battle Born State
Population: 2,700,551 (2010)
State Flower: Sagebrush
State Bird: Mountain bluebird
State Tree: Single-leaf piñon, bristlecone pine
State Song: "Home Means Nevada"
Motto: *All for Our Country*
Postal Code: NV

Fun Facts (2009)
Amusement Parks: 2
Toy Stores: 74
Pet and Pet Supply Stores: 75

Did You Know?

Nevada
- is the driest of the 50 states.
- is the location of Lake Mead and Lake Tahoe.
- is the location of Las Vegas, one of the fastest growing cities in the United States.
- was once part of Mexico; the Treaty of Guadalupe Hidalgo, which ended the Mexican War, granted the area to the United States.

Use the code below to learn about some interesting people, places, and events in Nevada.

1-S
2-G 5-M
3-U 6-Y
4-O 7-B
     8-I
     9-H

10-F 14-L
11-Z 15-D
12-N 16-W
13-E 17-V

18-X 22-Q
19-A 23-P
20-T 24-R
21-C 25-J
      26-K

first a railroad town, now, a gambling town __ __ __ __ __ __ __ __
14 19 1   17 13 2 19 1

Nevada's nickname __ __ __ __ __ __ __ __ __ __ __ __ __ __
20 9 13   1 8 14 17 13 24   1 20 19 20 13

a cowboy poet __ __ __ __ __ __ __ __ __ __ __ __ __ __
16 19 15 15 8 13   5 8 20 21 9 13 14 14

this holds water __ __ __ __ __ __ __ __ __
9 4 4 17 13 24   15 19 5

a backward name for a town __ __ __ __ __ __
19 15 19 17 13 12

Famous Nevadans

- Andre Agassi is a tennis player who won the US Open in 1994.
- Edna Purviance was born in Paradise Valley. She starred in more than 30 of Charlie Chaplin's movies.
- Sarah Winnemucca Hopkins was an American Indian who fought for American Indians' rights.
- Anne Martin was born in Empire City. She fought for the woman's right to vote.
- Jack Kramer was born in Las Vegas. He won the US Open in 1946 and 1947.
- Waddie Mitchell, born in Elko, is a cowboy poet.

State Greats

- Any adult can adopt a wild horse or burro in Nevada. The cost is $125 per horse and $75 per burro.
- There is a town in Nevada named Adaven. That is Nevada spelled backward.
- The largest cutthroat trout ever caught weighed 41 pounds. It was fished from Pyramid Lake in 1925.
- Nevada is the country's driest state. Less rain falls there than in any other state.
- The Hoover Dam is the second tallest concrete dam in the country.

New Hampshire

Longest Conga Line on Ice
February 27, 2011

A conga line is also called a snake dance because people move in single file in a line. A conga line is an easy way to walk or dance as a group. But, can you imagine joining a conga line on ice skates? That could be a challenge. If one person falls on the ice, the whole line might topple. But, it was easy skating for a group of students from Phillips Exeter Academy in Exeter, New Hampshire. A total of 259 students skated in single file, forming the Longest Conga Line on Ice.

The New Hampshire quarter features an image of the Old Man of the Mountain, a rock formation that resembled a man's face. Sadly, the rock formation fell from its perch in 2003.

State Facts

New Hampshire

★ Concord

Statehood: 6/21/1788
Rank: 9
Nickname: Granite State
Population: 1,316,470 (2010)
State Flower: Purple lilac
State Bird: Purple finch
State Tree: White birch
State Song: Old New Hampshire
Motto: *Live Free or Die*
Postal Code: NH

Fun Facts (2009)
Amusement Parks: 12
Toy Stores: 75
Pet and Pet Supply Stores: 62

Did You Know?

New Hampshire

- is known by its official trademark: the Old Man of the Mountain, a natural granite formation on Profile Mountain.
- is the state where, since 1920, the earliest presidential primary election has been held.
- is the home state of Franklin Pierce, the fourteenth president.
- is the birthplace of Alan Shepard, America's first astronaut in space.

Complete the crossword puzzle below.

Across

3 New Hampshire delegates were the first to vote on the _____ of Independence.

5 Sarah Josepha _____ wrote "Mary Had a Little Lamb."

6 New Hampshire is called the _____ State.

Down

1 Captain John _____ named New Hampshire.

2 The world's fastest winds were recorded on Mount _____.

4 The state's capital is _____.

7 In 1788, New Hampshire became the _____ state.

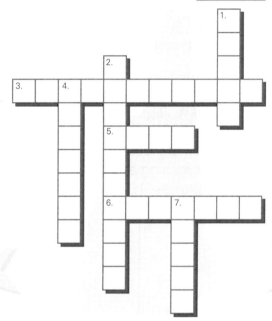

Famous New Hampshirites

- Daniel Webster was a famous lawyer, speaker, and statesman born in Franklin.
- Horace Greeley was the founder and publisher of the *New York Tribune*.
- Sarah Josepha Hale wrote "Mary Had a Little Lamb."
- Poet Robert Frost was born in California but considered Derry, New Hampshire, his home. He won the Pulitzer Prize four times.
- Edward A. and Marian Nevins MacDowell founded the MacDowell Colony for artists in Peterborough.

State Greats

- Franconia was home to "The Old Man of the Mountain," a stone ledge that looked like the side view of a face until it fell in 2003. It measured 40 feet from chin to forehead.
- The treaty ending the Russo-Japanese War was signed in Portsmouth in 1905.
- Every four years, New Hampshire holds the country's first presidential primary.
- The fastest winds in the world were recorded atop Mount Washington in 1934. The winds were recorded at 231 miles per hour.
- New Hampshire has the largest House of Representatives of any state in the country.

New Jersey

Longest Career as an Ice Cream Man
July 2009

There's no better sound on a hot summer day than the musical sound of an ice cream truck coming down the road. Kids and adults often drop what they are doing to run outside for an ice cream treat. Ice cream trucks have been popular for years. Just ask Charlie D'Angelo, of Clifton, New Jersey, who has been an ice cream man for 30 years. Since 1979, D'Angelo has been selling ice cream from his Iggy's Igloo ice cream truck. D'Angelo got his first ice cream delivery job when he was 12.

The scene on the New Jersey quarter dates back to the American Revolutionary War. It depicts George Washington's surprise crossing of the Delaware River on Christmas, 1776.

State Facts

New Jersey

★Trenton

Statehood: 12/18/1787
Rank: 3
Nickname: Garden State
Population: 8,791,894 (2010)
State Flower: Violet
State Bird: Eastern goldfinch
State Tree: Red oak
Motto: *Liberty and Prosperity*
Postal Code: NJ

Fun Facts (2009)
Amusement Parks: 24
Toy Stores: 280
Pet and Pet Supply Stores: 286

Did You Know?

New Jersey
- is nicknamed the "Garden State."
- is where Thomas Edison set up his laboratory and made many astounding discoveries and inventions.
- is the home state of Woodrow Wilson, the twenty-eighth president of the United States.
- is where, in 1524, Giovanni de Verrazzano explored the coast.
- is where, on June 6, 1933, the first drive-in movie theater in the United States opened.

Use the words in the Word Bank to find and circle the words about New Jersey in the word search below.

Word Bank   Cleveland   Hoboken   Princeton   Trenton   Morse
Hudson   Cooper   Sinatra   Washington   Edison

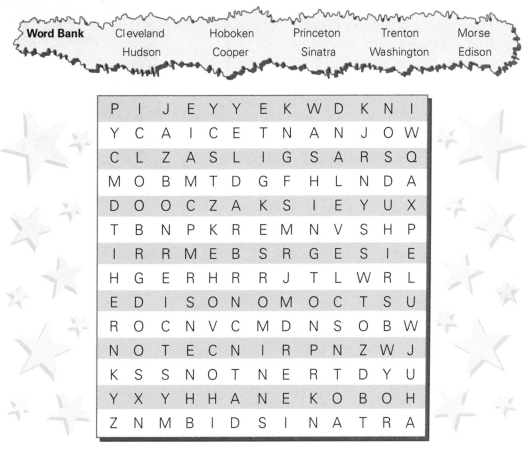

P	I	J	E	Y	Y	E	K	W	D	K	N	I
Y	C	A	I	C	E	T	N	A	N	J	O	W
C	L	Z	A	S	L	I	G	S	A	R	S	Q
M	O	B	M	T	D	G	F	H	L	N	D	A
D	O	O	C	Z	A	K	S	I	E	Y	U	X
T	B	N	P	K	R	E	M	N	V	S	H	P
I	R	R	M	E	B	S	R	G	E	S	I	E
H	G	E	R	H	R	R	J	T	L	W	R	L
E	D	I	S	O	N	O	M	O	C	T	S	U
R	O	C	N	V	C	M	D	N	S	O	B	W
N	O	T	E	C	N	I	R	P	N	Z	W	J
K	S	S	N	O	T	N	E	R	T	D	Y	U
Y	X	Y	H	H	A	N	E	K	O	B	O	H
Z	N	M	B	I	D	S	I	N	A	T	R	A

Famous New Jerseyans

- Frank Sinatra, a famous singer and actor, was born in Hoboken.
- Aaron Burr was vice president of the United States under Thomas Jefferson.
- James Fenimore Cooper wrote novels about western expansion.
- Walt Whitman was a famous poet and writer.
- Grover Cleveland was the twenty-second and twenty-fourth president of the United States.
- Bruce Springsteen is a well-known musician and singer.

State Greats

- The science of studying dinosaur fossils began in 1858. Scientists discovered the first nearly complete skeleton of a dinosaur in Haddonfield.
- Paterson was the first planned industrial city in America.
- Princeton University is one of America's most respected universities. Albert Einstein did some of his research there.
- Thomas Edison invented his electric light in his laboratory at Menlo Park.
- Samuel Morse invented the telegraph near his home in Morristown.
- Hoboken was the site of the first pro baseball game in 1846.

Highest Altitude Reached by Helium-filled Party Balloons
August 4, 2001

Have you ever heard of a sport called cluster ballooning? This is when a person is harnessed to a cluster, or bunch, of balloons inflated with helium. Then, the person is released up, up, and away! Mike Howard (UK) and Steve Davis (USA) harnessed themselves to 1,400 helium-filled latex toy balloons. Howard and Davis rose to a height of 18,300 feet near Albuquerque, New Mexico. Albuquerque is often called the Balloon Capital of the World, making this a perfect location for a ballooning record.

The New Mexico quarter features a topographical image of the state. A Zia sun symbol marks the location of the state capital city, Santa Fe. The Zia sun represents the giver of all good.

State Facts

New Mexico
★ Santa Fe

Statehood: 1/6/1912
Rank: 47
Nickname: Land of Enchantment
Population: 2,059,179 (2010)
State Flower: Yucca flower
State Bird: Roadrunner
State Tree: Two-needle piñon
State Song: "O, Fair New Mexico"
Motto: *It Grows As It Goes*
Postal Code: NM

Fun Facts (2009)
Amusement Parks: 2
Toy Stores: 51
Pet and Pet Supply Stores: 54

Did You Know?

New Mexico
- is separated from Mexico by the Rio Grande.
- is the home of Carlsbad Caverns National Park.
- is the site of El Camino Real, the oldest road built by Europeans in the United States.
- was explored by Coronado, the Spanish explorer who searched for a legendary lost city of gold, in 1540–1542.
- is where, on July 16, 1945, the world's first atomic bomb exploded.

Read the clues. Unscramble the words about New Mexico.

a city founded
in 1706 __ __ __ __ __ __ __ __ __ __ __   Q U Q U E E R A L B U

the capital __ __ __ __ __   __ __   E F T A S A N

last name of an artist
who painted New Mexico __ __ __ __ __ __ __   E E F E F K O '

"the big river"

__ __ __   __ __ __   __ __ __ __ __ __   E H T   I R O   A R N E G D

Write the first letter of each word in the puzzle.

__ __ __ __

Unscramble the letters to find the name of a city in New Mexico.

__ __ __ __

Famous New Mexicans

- Dionisio Chavez was the first Mexican American senator.
- Georgia O'Keeffe painted the New Mexican landscape and lived on a ranch near Taos.
- Maria Martinez, born in San Ildefonso, created traditional Pueblo Indian pottery.
- Charles Bent was the first governor of New Mexico.
- Elizabeth Garrett wrote the state song in English in 1917.
- Amadeo Lucero wrote the Spanish state song "Asi Es Nuevo Méjico" in 1971.
- Buffalo Bill started his first western road show from Cimarron.

State Greats

- Scientists developed the nuclear bomb in Los Alamos and tested it at the White Sands Missile Range.
- Visitors can walk a three-mile underground trail at Carlsbad Caverns National Park.
- The International UFO Museum and Research Center is in Roswell.
- At Taos Pueblo, outside the city of Taos, Pueblo Indians still live in adobe dwellings.
- Capulin Volcano National Monument has a 1,000-foot volcano. The volcano is no longer active and is now a monument.
- The Rio Grande is one of the longest rivers in North America.

Largest Donation of School Supplies in 24 Hours
August 4, 2010

Students go through a lot of school supplies in a year. Just think about all of the pencils, pens, notebooks, crayons, paper, paint, tape, scissors, tissues, and more. The list is long. Many schools have supply drives to fill the many needs of classrooms. But, in August 2010, a company called Avery Dennison donated 8,651 pounds of school supplies to the Adolph S. Ochs School in New York, New York. The company donated enough school supplies to fill a full-size school bus!

The New York quarter features an image of the Statue of Liberty. "Lady Liberty," as she is also called, was a gift from France. She has proudly stood in New York City's harbor since 1886.

State Facts

New York

Albany★

Statehood: 7/26/1788
Rank: 11
Nicknames: Empire State, Excelsior State
Population: 19,378,102 (2010)
State Flower: Rose
State Bird: Eastern bluebird
State Tree: Sugar maple
State Song: "I Love New York"
Motto: *Ever Upward*
Postal Code: NY

Fun Facts (2009)
Amusement Parks: 33
Toy Stores: 544
Pet and Pet Supply Stores: 632

Did You Know?

New York
- is the home of Lake Placid, site of the 1932 and 1980 Winter Olympic games.
- is the home of the United States Military Academy at West Point.
- is the "birthplace" of baseball and home of the National Baseball Hall of Fame at Cooperstown.
- is where President McKinley was assassinated while attending the Pan-American Exposition in 1901.
- is where George Washington first took the oath of office as the nation's president.

Read each clue. Use the code to find the answers.

1-A	5-E	9-I	13-X	17-K	21-U	25-Y
2-G	6-J	10-P	14-D	18-R	22-V	26-F
3-C	7-B	11-M	15-O	19-Z	23-W	
4-N	8-H	12-L	16-S	20-T	24-Q	

first name of New York's famous actor and director

○ __ __ __ __
23 15 15 14 25

a river named for an explorer

○ __ __ __ __ __
8 21 14 16 15 4

first name of first explorer

__ ○ __ __ ○ __ __ __
2 9 15 22 1 4 4 9

used to be called Fort Orange

○ __ __ ○ __ __
1 12 7 1 4 25

home of George Eastman

__ __ __ ○ __ __ __ ○ __ __
18 15 3 8 5 16 20 5 8

Unscramble the circled letters to write the name of the famous Iroquois leader.

__ __ __ __ __ __ __ __

Famous New Yorkers

- Hiawatha was an Iroquois leader and peacemaker who helped set up the Iroquois Federation.
- Franklin D. Roosevelt was born in Hyde Park and became the thirty-second president of the United States.
- James Baldwin wrote books about African Americans and lived in New York City.
- George Gershwin wrote music for orchestras.
- Elizabeth Ann Seton was a saint and founded the Sisters of Charity.
- Herman Melville is famous for writing the book *Moby Dick*.

State Greats

- From 1892 to 1954, millions of people came to America through Ellis Island. It is now a museum.
- More than 500,000 gallons of water flow over Niagara Falls every second. It is one of the largest, most famous falls in the world. It is in both Canada and the United States.
- The first American women's rights convention was held in Seneca Falls.
- The Kodak camera was invented by George Eastman in Rochester.
- New York City has the country's largest art museum, the Metropolitan Museum of Art.
- New York City was the first capital city of the United States.

North Carolina

Most Volunteer Hours Worked
March 5, 2010

Don Moss has been called the "Energizer Bunny of Volunteers" by some of the people who have worked with him. To earn the record for Most Volunteer Hours Worked, he volunteered for a total of 46,853 hours at Wake Forest University Baptist Medical Center in Winston-Salem, North Carolina. Moss worked about 40 hours per week. He worked in the hospital gift shop, delivered flowers, and took letters to patients. He decided to volunteer after getting hurt and landing at Wake Forest Baptist as a patient. Volunteering is Moss's way of giving back. And, he's not done yet!

The North Carolina quarter features an image of the historic first flight of Orville and Wilbur Wright's airplane in 1903. The airplane stayed up for 12 seconds and flew about 120 feet.

State Facts

Statehood: 11/21/1789
Rank: 12
Nicknames: Tar Heel State, Old North State
Population: 9,535,483 (2010)
State Flower: Dogwood flower
State Bird: Cardinal
State Tree: Pine
State Song: "The Old North State"
Motto: *To Be Rather Than to Seem*
Postal Code: NC

Fun Facts (2009)
Amusement Parks: 18
Toy Stores: 247
Pet and Pet Supply Stores: 215

Did You Know?

North Carolina
- is the location of both the Blue Ridge and the Great Smoky Mountains.
- is the location of Cape Hatteras, sometimes called the "Graveyard of the Atlantic"—many shipwrecks have occurred nearby.
- is where, in 1903, the Wright brothers launched the world's first successful airplane flight near Kitty Hawk.
- is the location of Ocracoke Island, where Blackbeard the pirate had a hideout.

Read the clues. Unscramble the words about North Carolina.

she was known for entertaining   — — — — — — —   N M D I O S A

first flyers   — — — — — —   G T W R H I

a famous jazz musician   — — — —   K M N O

a great slam dunker   — — — — — —   J N D O A R

the first African American
to serve in the Senate   — — — — — —   V S E R E L

Unscramble the letters to find North Carolina's missing settlers.

S L T O Y L O C N O

— — — —   — — — — — —

Famous North Carolinians

- James K. Polk was the eleventh president of the United States.
- Andrew Johnson was the seventeenth president of the United States.
- Levi Coffin was a leader of the Underground Railroad.
- Dolley Madison was famous for entertaining as first lady.
- Hiram Revels was the first African American to serve in the US Senate.
- Michael Jordan is one of the greatest players in the history of the NBA.
- Thelonious Monk is a famous jazz musician.

State Greats

- The world's largest mill for weaving denim is in Greensboro.
- The highest eastern American peak is Mount Mitchell.
- North Carolina is the home of the Charlotte Bobcats and the Carolina Panthers.
- North Carolina is a major producer of furniture.
- The University of North Carolina at Chapel Hill is one of the first state-supported universities in the country.
- A lighthouse was installed at Cape Hatteras because of the great number of shipwrecks there.

North Dakota

Most People Making Snow Angels Simultaneously
February 17, 2007

Thousands of people—adults, children, and even snowplow drivers—lay in the snow and made snow angels. The participants flapped their arms and legs to set a world record. One of the participants made her first snow angel ever. It was on her 99th birthday. The 8,962 people broke the record at the North Dakota State Capitol grounds in Bismarck, North Dakota. The State Historical Society of North Dakota organized the record-breaking event.

The North Dakota quarter features an image of two bison grazing in the Badlands. Large herds of bison roamed free in the Badlands until the 1860s.

State Facts

North Dakota

★Bismarck

Statehood: 11/2/1889
Rank: 39
Nickname: Peace Garden State
Population: 672,591 (2010)
State Flower: Wild prairie rose
State Bird: Western meadowlark
State Tree: American elm
State Song: "North Dakota Hymn"
Motto: *Liberty and Union, Now and Forever, One and Inseparable*
Postal Code: ND

Fun Facts (2009)
Amusement Parks: 1
Toy Stores: 29
Pet and Pet Supply Stores: 18

Did You Know?

North Dakota

- has two other nicknames: "Flickertail State" and "Sioux State."
- has a high production of barley and wheat.
- is home to several American Indian groups including the Sioux, Hidatsa, Ojibwa, and Cheyenne.
- measured an all-time low temperature of -60°F on February 15, 1936.

Anna wrote a report about her summer trip to North Dakota. Fill in the letters that she left out.

★ ★

My Summer trip to ___orth Dakota

___orth Dak___ta is a big state. My family and I didn't see everything, but here are the things I liked best.

We visited the ___ndian ___etroglyphs at Writing ___ock near ___rosby. It was fun to imagine the American ___ndians who made these drawings. I can't believe how old the drawings are!

We also saw the United Stat___s Strategic ___ir ___ommand at Grand ___orks. They have a lot of neat planes!

For natural beauty, the ___ ___eodore ___oosevelt National Memorial Park was the best. We went on a long hike.

I think you'd love North Dakota.

Anna Turner

Unscramble the letters you have written to find the name of the railroad that brought settlers to North Dakota.

___ ___ ___ ___ ___ ___ ___ ___ ___   ___ ___ ___ ___ ___ ___ ___

Famous North Dakotans

- Sitting Bull was the leader of the Sioux.
- Lawrence Welk was a singer and a musician.
- Peggy Lee was a singer.
- Angie Dickinson acted in popular movies and TV shows.
- Running Antelope was pictured on one of the earlier versions of the five-dollar bill.
- D. H. Houston invented the roll film for photography.
- Konrad Elias Birkbough discovered a treatment for the skin disease erysipelas.

State Greats

- North Dakota has two United States Strategic Air Commands, one at Grand Forks and one at Minot.
- White Butte is 3,506 feet above sea level. It is the highest point in North Dakota.
- The Theodore Roosevelt National Memorial Park is named for President Roosevelt.
- Visitors can see ancient American Indian petroglyphs at the Writing Rock near Crosby.
- History buffs can celebrate at the "Pioneer Days at Bonanzaville" each year in West Fargo.

Most Neckties Worn at Once
December 9, 2010

Jason Handman worked at TV station CBS-W010 in Cleveland, Ohio. Usually, he could be seen on camera offering the day's weather report. Handman is a meteorologist. But, on December 9, 2010, Handman himself became part of a news story. He set a world record for wearing the most neckties at one time. He placed 131 ties around his neck, one at a time, and tied them in a knot. The station aired his record-setting attempt live on the 6:00 evening news.

The Ohio quarter celebrates the state's aviation triumphs. The biplane and an astronaut on either side of the state's outline symbolize Ohio's role in air and space advancement.

State Facts

Statehood: 3/1/1803
Rank: 17
Nickname: Buckeye State
Population: 11,536,504 (2010)
State Flower: Scarlet carnation
State Bird: Cardinal
State Tree: Buckeye
State Song: "Beautiful Ohio"
Motto: *With God, All Things Are Possible*
Postal Code: OH

Fun Facts (2009)
Amusement Parks: 23
Toy Stores: 311
Pet and Pet Supply Stores: 334

Did You Know?

Ohio
- was named after an Iroquois word meaning "beautiful."
- is known as the "Buckeye State" after a tree of the same name.
- was the first state admitted to the Union from the Northwest Territory.
- is the birthplace of seven presidents.
- is one of the nation's leading industrial states. Important manufacturing centers are located in or near a number of Ohio's major cities.

Next to each sentence write a _T_ if the statement is true or an _F_ if the statement is false.

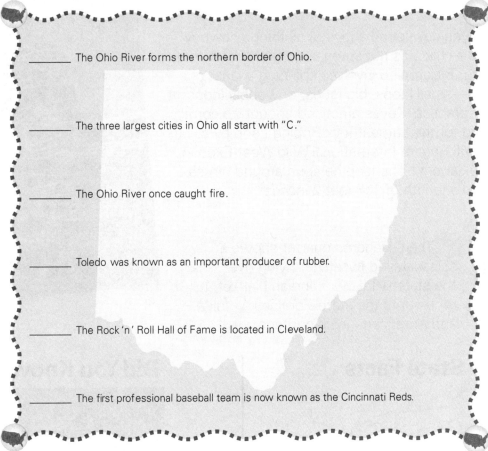

_____ The Ohio River forms the northern border of Ohio.

_____ The three largest cities in Ohio all start with "C."

_____ The Ohio River once caught fire.

_____ Toledo was known as an important producer of rubber.

_____ The Rock 'n' Roll Hall of Fame is located in Cleveland.

_____ The first professional baseball team is now known as the Cincinnati Reds.

Famous Ohioans

- John Glenn was the first American to orbit Earth. He also returned to space when he was 77.
- Presidents Ulysses S. Grant, Rutherford B. Hayes, James A. Garfield, Benjamin Harrison, William McKinley, William H. Taft, and Warren G. Harding came from Ohio.
- Steven Spielberg made movies such as _E.T._, _Raiders of the Lost Ark_, and _Schindler's List_.
- Neil Armstrong was the first person to walk on the moon.
- Maya Lin designed the Vietnam Veterans Memorial in Washington, DC.

State Greats

- The Cincinnati Red Stockings, now the Reds, became the first professional baseball team.
- Akron was once known as the "Rubber Capital of the World."
- The Rock 'n' Roll Hall of Fame is located in Cleveland.
- The Pro Football Hall of Fame is located in Canton.
- The Cuyahoga River, near Lake Erie, was once so polluted that it caught fire. Today, it is a clean river.
- Oberlin College was the first to educate men and women together.

Oklahoma

Largest Trick Roping Loop by a Male
April 22, 2006

Charlie Keyes developed a love of all things cowboy when he was a child. It's not surprising that he later took up trick roping. Trick roping involves spinning a lariat or a lasso in loops—small loops, big loops, or wobbly loops! It takes a lot of practice. Keyes practiced enough to corral a world record for the Largest Trick Roping Loop by a Male at the Will Rogers International Wild West Expo in Claremore, Oklahoma. The loop he spun around himself was fed out to a length of 107 feet 2 inches.

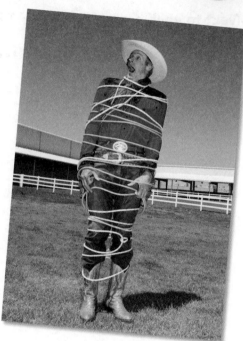

The Oklahoma quarter shows a scissor-tailed flycatcher flying over the state wildflower, Indian blanket. It represents the state's prairies, wildlife, and American Indian heritage.

State Facts

Oklahoma
★ Oklahoma City

Statehood: 11/16/1907
Rank: 46
Nickname: Sooner State
Population: 3,751,351 (2010)
State Flower: Oklahoma rose
State Bird: Scissor-tailed flycatcher
State Tree: Redbud
State Song: "Oklahoma"
Motto: *Labor Conquers All Things*
Postal Code: OK

Fun Facts (2009)
Amusement Parks: 9
Toy Stores: 91
Pet and Pet Supply Stores: 77

Did You Know?

Oklahoma

- is named after words from the American Indian Choctaw language that mean "red people."
- is the home of the National Cowboy & Western Heritage Museum.
- is the location of the Chisholm Trail, which was used by cowboys to drive millions of cattle from Texas to Kansas.
- has working oil wells on the grounds of the state capitol building.

Read the clues. Unscramble the words about Oklahoma.

This city has an oil well.

_ _ _ _ _ _ _ _   _ _ _ _

A K I M L H O A T O C Y

This rock is mostly found in Oklahoma.

_ _ _ _ _   _ _ _ _

R B I T E O A S E R

an American Indian tribe that lived in Oklahoma

_ _ _ _ _ _ _ _ _

H C A C K A S I W

the Spanish explorer who came to Oklahoma

_ _ _ _ _ _ _

D R O N O C O A

the terrible journey of the American Indians

_ _ _ _ _ _ _   _ _ _ _ _

F E R A L T O I R S A T

Famous Oklahomans

- Will Rogers was a famous comedian and entertainer.
- Mickey Mantle was a star baseball player for the New York Yankees.
- Woody Guthrie was a folk singer, guitarist, and composer.
- Ralph Ellison was a well-known African American writer and author of *The Invisible Man*.
- Alice Mary Robertson was the first woman from Oklahoma to be elected to the US House of Representatives.
- Maria Tallchief was a classical dancer and a prima ballerina for the New York City Ballet.

State Greats

- Oklahoma City has the only capitol building that has operating oil wells on its grounds.
- US Highway 69 follows Texas Road, one of the earliest routes through Indian Territory to Texas.
- Barite rose rock is found mostly in Oklahoma. Cherokee legend says the rocks stand for the blood of the braves and the tears of the maidens who made the "Trail of Tears" journey.
- Oklahoma has 39 tribal nations that are recognized by the federal government as sovereign.

Oregon

Largest Sea Cave

The Sea Lion Caves on the Oregon coastline are home to, well, sea lions. About 200 sea lions live there in a large cave. Sea lions can be very large. Although a pup may weigh 50 pounds at birth, adult females can grow to be 800 pounds. Adult males might weigh as much as 2,500 pounds. So, it's a good thing the Sea Lion Caves are so vast. The main cavern is the Largest Sea Cave ever, measuring 310 feet long, 165 feet wide, and about 50 feet high.

The Oregon quarter features an image of Wizard Island at Crater Lake. Thousands of years ago, the lake formed in a former volcano crater and is one of the deepest lakes in the world. Wizard Island, made from volcanic ash, rises from the middle of the lake.

State Facts

Oregon
★ Salem

Statehood: 2/14/1859
Rank: 33
Nickname: Beaver State
Population: 3,831,074 (2010)
State Flower: Oregon grape
State Bird: Western meadowlark
State Tree: Douglas fir
State Song: "Oregon, My Oregon"
Motto: *She Flies with Her Own Wings*
Postal Code: OR

Fun Facts (2009)
Amusement Parks: 2
Toy Stores: 169
Pet and Pet Supply Stores: 168

Did You Know?

Oregon
- is bordered on the north by the Columbia River.
- is the location of Crater Lake—at 1,932 feet deep, it is the deepest lake in the United States.
- is the location of Deschutes National Forest, which has the largest forest of lava-cast trees in the world.
- is the location of Fort Clatsop, where Lewis and Clark and their band of explorers spent the terrible winter of 1805–1806.

Read the clues. Complete the words about Oregon.

an explorer's fort __ __ __ __ __ O __

a children's author __ __ __ __ R __

Chief Joseph's tribe __ __ __ __ E __ __ __

he explored the Columbia River G __ __ __

Pauling won two of these prizes __ O __ __ __

a Nike shoe man __ N __ __ __ __

Famous Oregonians

- Barbara Roberts was Oregon's first female governor.
- Raymond Carver was an author and a poet.
- Chief Joseph was a great Nez Percé leader.
- Phil Knight founded Nike, Inc.
- Gary Payton is a professional basketball player.
- Mark O. Hatfield was a governor and a state senator.
- Linus Pauling won Nobel prizes for chemistry and peace.
- Beverly Cleary won the Newbery Medal for children's literature.

State Greats

- A volcanic explosion of Mount Mazama created Crater Lake. Crater Lake is 1,932 feet deep, the deepest lake in the United States.
- Oregon Dunes National Recreation Area contains miles of seaside sand dunes for family enjoyment.
- Hells Canyon on the Snake River is 7,900 feet deep—deeper than the Grand Canyon.
- Ashland is home to the annual Oregon Shakespeare Festival.
- Hundreds of thousands of birds migrating along the Pacific "Flyway" stop in the national wildlife refuges near Upper Klamath Lake.

Largest Individual Chocolate
July 7, 2007

The Hershey Company makes millions and millions of Hershey's Kisses every day at its factories. These chocolates are very popular. Many people find it hard to eat just one! Chocolate lovers might eat one and then another, and so on. But, it is hard to imagine that anyone could eat the entire Kiss that Hershey's made to celebrate the company's 100th anniversary. The Kiss weighed a sweet 30,540 pounds. The company proudly displayed it at Chocolate World in Hershey, Pennsylvania.

The Pennsylvania quarter shows a keystone and the Commonwealth statue. The keystone was a state symbol during the US Civil War. The statue represents justice and mercy.

State Facts

Pennsylvania

Harrisburg
★

Statehood: 12/12/1787
Rank: 2
Nickname: Keystone State
Population: 12,702,379 (2010)
State Flower: Mountain laurel
State Bird: Ruffed grouse
State Tree: Hemlock
State Song: "Pennsylvania"
Motto: *Virtue, Liberty, and Independence*
Postal Code: PA

Fun Facts (2009)
Amusement Parks: 29
Toy Stores: 351
Pet and Pet Supply Stores: 379

Did You Know?

Pennsylvania

- has another nickname: the "Quaker State." It refers to the religion of William Penn and other Quakers who settled in the state.
- is the location of the world's largest chocolate factory.
- is where the Declaration of Independence was signed in 1776.
- was, in 1681, a large land grant offered by King Charles II to William Penn.

Read the clues about Pennsylvania. Use the code to find the answers.

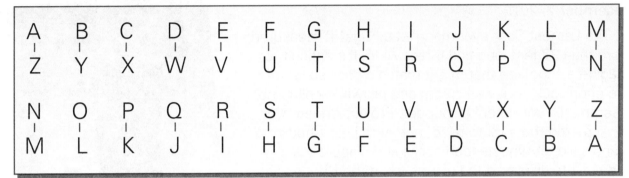

A	B	C	D	E	F	G	H	I	J	K	L	M
Z	Y	X	W	V	U	T	S	R	Q	P	O	N

N	O	P	Q	R	S	T	U	V	W	X	Y	Z
M	L	K	J	I	H	G	F	E	D	C	B	A

one of the first people living in Pennsylvania __ __ __ Ⓞ Ⓞ __ __ __
R I L J F L R H

an English ruler who gave land to William Penn Ⓞ __ __ __ __ __ __ Ⓞ __ Ⓞ __
P R M T   X S Z I O V H

an Ottawa chief who fought England __ __ __ __ __ Ⓞ __
K L M G R Z X

a comic and actor born in Philadelphia __ __ Ⓞ __ __
X L H Y B

Unscramble the circled letters. Find the name of the settlers who followed William Penn to Pennsylvania.

__ __ __ __ __ __ __ __

Famous Pennsylvanians

- James Buchanan was the fifteenth president.
- General George Marshall, born in Uniontown, created the Marshall Plan.
- Louisa May Alcott, born in Germantown, wrote *Little Women*.
- Mary Cassatt, from Allegheny City, was a modern painter.
- Thomas Eakins, born in Philadelphia, was an oil painter.
- Margaret Mead was an anthropologist and a writer.
- Bill Cosby, another Philadelphian, is an actor and a comic.

State Greats

- Little League baseball started in Williamsport in 1939.
- The world's largest chocolate factory is in Hershey.
- When coal was discovered near Pittsburgh, the state became a leading coal producer.
- Lincoln gave his famous Gettysburg Address in Gettysburg in 1863.
- In 1794, Pennsylvania built the country's first turnpike. This road connected Philadelphia and Lancaster.
- Philadelphia was the nation's capital city after New York and before Washington, DC.

Largest Sock
December 2, 2011

The Largest Sock ever made was huge! It measured more than 32 feet long and 8 feet wide. It's difficult to imagine a shoe size that might match a sock so large! The enormous sock was cream and brown in color and resembled a sock monkey puppet. Project Undercover, Inc., created the sock to raise money to help Rhode Island children who needed socks and diapers. Participants displayed the giant sock at the Rhode Island Convention Center in Providence, Rhode Island.

The Rhode Island quarter celebrates the state's 400-plus miles of coastline and favorite sport—sailing. The featured sailboat skims through Narragansett Bay, where others may swim or fish.

State Facts

Rhode Island
★Providence

Statehood: 5/29/1790
Rank: 13
Nickname: The Ocean State, Little Rhody
Population: 1,052,567 (2010)
State Flower: Violet
State Bird: Rhode Island Red chicken
State Tree: Red maple
State Song: "Rhode Island's It for Me"
Motto: *Hope*
Postal Code: RI

Fun Facts (2009)
Amusement Parks: 2
Toy Stores: 35
Pet and Pet Supply Stores: 42

Did You Know?

Rhode Island
- is the smallest of the 50 states.
- is cut almost in half by Narragansett Bay.
- ranks first in the nation in the production of costume jewelry.
- is where a permanent European settlement was founded, in 1636, by Roger Williams. He was banished from Massachusetts because of his religious beliefs.
- was first to declare its independence from Britain on May 4, 1776.

Write the letter from column B next to the matching phrase in column A.

 A

 B

1. _____ founder of Rhode Island

2. _____ capital city

3. _____ US general during American Revolution

4. _____ site of America's first cotton mill

5. _____ George Washington's portrait painter

A Nathanael Greene

B Pawtucket

C Providence

D Gilbert Stuart

E Roger Williams

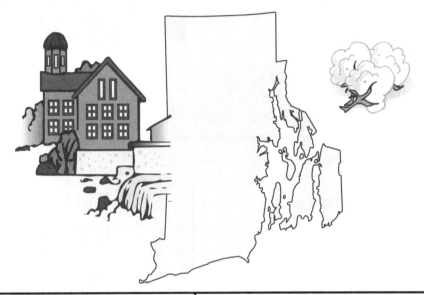

Famous Rhode Islanders

- Nathanael Greene was a general during the American Revolution.
- Oliver Hazard Perry was a hero and US Naval officer in the War of 1812.
- Matthew Calbraith Perry opened up Japanese ports to western trade.
- Anne Hutchinson protested against the religious leaders of Massachusetts.
- Gilbert Stuart painted a famous portrait of George Washington.
- Ida Lewis was a lighthouse keeper who saved many lives.
- Napoleon "Nap" Lajoie was named to the Baseball Hall of Fame.

State Greats

- Slater Mill, America's first cotton mill, opened in Pawtucket in 1790.
- Rhode Island is considered a major hub of the American jewelry industry. Nehemiah Dodge developed a way to cover metal with a thin layer of gold or silver. Before his discovery, jewelry was made out of pure gold or silver and only the rich could afford to buy it.
- During the mid-nineteenth century, many wealthy families built mansions and vacationed in Newport.
- Today, Block Island is a favorite vacation spot.

Largest Picture Mosaic Formed by People
December 3, 2011

When friends and family found out about five-year-old Ansley McEvoy's life-threatening illness, they wanted to do something to make her smile. Ansley loves greeting cards. So, the group decided to make a giant picture mosaic card of one of her drawings. The drawing showed her family under a rainbow. A total of 1,458 people held up pieces to make the giant picture mosaic at Blackbaud Stadium on Daniel Island, South Carolina. The mosaic measured about 81 feet high by 108 feet wide.

The South Carolina quarter features an image of the state's outline, as well as various state symbols, including the state tree, bird, and flower.

State Facts

South Carolina
★Columbia

Statehood: 5/23/1788
Rank: 8
Nickname: Palmetto State
Population: 4,625,364 (2010)
State Flower: Yellow jessamine
State Bird: Carolina wren
State Tree: Palmetto
State Song: "Carolina," "South Carolina on My Mind"
Motto: *While I Breathe, I Hope*
Postal Code: SC

Fun Facts (2009)
Amusement Parks: 12
Toy Stores: 97
Pet and Pet Supply Stores: 113

Did You Know?

South Carolina
- was originally named after King Charles II of England.
- is nicknamed the "Palmetto State."
- is the location of popular resorts including Myrtle Beach and Hilton Head Island.
- was first seen by a European, Francisco Gordillo, in 1521.
- is where the first shots of the Civil War were fired.

Read the clues. Then, unscramble the words about South Carolina.

one of the first British settlements

— — — — — — — — — —   L C H E S A T O R N

a popular vacation beach

— — — — — — —   — — — — —   T M L R Y E   E C B A H

a state bordering South Carolina

— — — — — — —   O E G G A R I

where the Civil War started

— — — —   — — — — — —   T R F O   R U E M S T

a vacation spot and an island

— — — — — —   — — — —   O H T I L N   A D E H   S N I L D A
— — — — — —

where the governor works

— — — — — — — —   A C M L U B O I

Famous South Carolinians

- Jesse Jackson is a civil rights leader.
- James "Strom" Thurmond was governor of South Carolina and a US senator.
- Larry Doby became the second African American in Major League Baseball.
- Pat Conroy wrote novels based on his childhood in South Carolina.
- John Birks "Dizzy" Gillespie was a trumpet player who helped create the "bebop" style of jazz.
- Althea Gibson was an African American tennis player who dominated the sport in 1957 and 1958.

State Greats

- In 1861, South Carolina became the first state to leave the United States of America during the Civil War.
- The first shots of the Civil War were fired at Fort Sumter.
- The Fireproof Building is the first fireproof building in the nation.
- Greenville is a large business district in the northwest.
- The colony known as Carolina was divided into North Carolina and South Carolina in 1710.

South Dakota

Largest and Most Complete Tyrannosaurus Rex Skeleton
August 12, 1990

A boy named Sue? Maybe. No one knows whether this *Tyrannosaurus rex* skeleton is from a male or female dinosaur. The skeleton is named after Sue Hendrickson, the fossil hunter who found it in South Dakota. "Sue" measures 13 feet tall and 42 feet long. The skeleton has bird-like feet and massive legs. The skull itself weighs about 600 pounds! Sue's huge jaw holds 58 sharp teeth, each measuring 7.5 to 12 inches long. Sue is currently on display at The Field Museum in Chicago, Illinois.

The South Dakota quarter shows Mount Rushmore, where the faces of four American presidents are sculpted. A Chinese ring-necked pheasant, the state bird, soars overhead.

State Facts

South Dakota
★Pierre

Statehood: 11/2/1889
Rank: 40
Nickname: Mount Rushmore State
Population: 814,180 (2010)
State Flower: Pasque
State Bird: Chinese ring-necked pheasant
State Tree: Black Hills spruce
State Song: "Hail, South Dakota"
Motto: *Under God, the People Rule*
Postal Code: SD

Fun Facts (2009)
Amusement Parks: 3
Toy Stores: 35
Pet and Pet Supply Stores: 19

Did You Know?

South Dakota

- is also known as the "Coyote State."
- is roughly divided in half by the Missouri River.
- is the location of Mount Rushmore, the famous monument to four presidents: Washington, Jefferson, Lincoln, and Theodore Roosevelt.
- is the home of Homestake Mine, the oldest gold mine in the world.
- did not grow much in population until 1874, when gold was discovered in the Black Hills.

Draw a line to match the dates on the left with the events on the right.

1889 ★   ★ The La Vérendrye brothers reach the Missouri River.

1743 ★   ★ Massacre at Wounded Knee Creek kills 300 Sioux.

1876 ★   ★ South Dakota becomes a state, and the Sioux are moved onto reservations.

1874 ★   ★ Crazy Horse, Sitting Bull, and Gall attack at Little Bighorn.

1890 ★   ★ Gold is found in the Black Hills.

Famous South Dakotans

- Sitting Bull was a Sioux warrior.
- Zitkala-Sa was a Sioux author who lived on the Yankton Reservation.
- Harvey Dunn painted pictures of World War I and life in South Dakota.
- Allen Neuharth, of Eureka, is the founder of the newspaper *USA Today*.
- Tom Brokaw, a national news anchorman, was born in Webster.
- Sparky Anderson, from Bridgewater, is one of baseball's greatest managers.
- Hubert Humphrey, of Wallace, was vice president and founder of the Peace Corps.

State Greats

- Wall Drug, a huge tourist attraction in Wall, has advertised "free ice water" since 1931.
- Badlands National Park's colorful hills and canyons stretch for almost 400 square miles.
- Mount Rushmore National Memorial graces the hills of South Dakota.
- Jewel Cave and Wind Cave of the Black Hills are two of the longest caves in the world.
- The Crazy Horse Monument near Mount Rushmore will be the largest sculpture in the world when completed.

Largest T-Shirt
June 11, 2011

Most stores carry T-shirts in sizes small, medium, large, and extra large. But, there has never been a label made for a T-shirt this humongous. The T-shirt was almost as large as a football field! The world's Largest T-shirt measured 281.3 feet long and 180.9 feet wide. The T-shirt's creators displayed it at Centennial Park during the 40th annual Country Music Association's Music Festival in Nashville, Tennessee. Plans were to recycle the shirt and make 12,000 shirts to donate to Nashville's school music programs.

The Tennessee quarter celebrates the state's strong musical heritage. The instruments featured represent the most popular music there: bluegrass, country, and blues.

State Facts

Tennessee
★ Nashville

Statehood: 6/1/1796
Rank: 16
Nickname: Volunteer State
Population: 6,346,105 (2010)
State Flower: Iris
State Bird: Mockingbird
State Tree: Tulip poplar
State Song: "Tennessee Waltz"
Motto: *Agriculture and Commerce*
Postal Code: TN

Fun Facts (2009)
Amusement Parks: 7
Toy Stores: 157
Pet and Pet Supply Stores: 124

Did You Know?

Tennessee
- is the location of the Grand Ole Opry, the most famous country music center in the world.
- is the location of Graceland, the estate of Elvis Presley, which attracts thousands of visitors each year.
- is the birthplace of three presidents: Andrew Jackson, James K. Polk, and Andrew Johnson.
- is where the Battle of Shiloh, an important battle of the Civil War, was fought.

Read the clues. Write the answers on the lines. Then, read the boxed letters to find out where the Grand Ole Opry is.

1. What national park is found in Tennessee?

2. Who developed an alphabet?

3. What entertainer is known as the King of Rock and Roll?

4. Who wrote historical novels?

5. What is the name of the war hero Gary Cooper portrayed?

6. On what Cherokee word is the name Tennessee based?

7. What was the first name suggested for Tennessee?

8. Who was the eleventh president of the United States?

9. Who was the "coonskin cap" frontiersman?

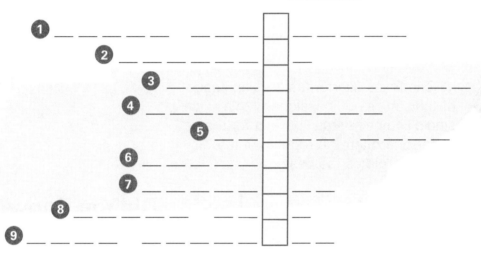

Where is the Grand Ole Opry radio show? _____

Famous Tennesseeans

- Davy Crockett was the legendary "coonskin cap" frontiersman and politician.
- Actor Gary Cooper won an Oscar for his portrayal of World War I hero Alvin York.
- Sequoyah, a Cherokee silversmith, developed an alphabet for the Cherokee language.
- Author Alex Haley wrote historical novels.
- Elvis Presley, who lived in Memphis, was considered the King of Rock and Roll.
- Actress Oprah Winfrey, who lived in Nashville as a teenager, owns a TV network.
- James Polk was the eleventh president.

State Greats

- The Tennessee Aquarium in Chattanooga has the largest freshwater aquarium in the country.
- The National Civil Rights Museum in Memphis at the Lorraine Motel is in honor of Martin Luther King Jr. He was killed in the motel.
- Bristol is the birthplace of "Country Music."
- The Grand Ole Opry radio show has run continuously since 1925.
- More people visit the Great Smoky Mountains National Park than any other national park in the United States. It is named for the bluish haze that covers the mountains.

Longest Horns on a Texas Longhorn Steer

Gibralter is a red Texas Longhorn steer that truly lives up to his name. Gibralter's horns are the longest in the world. They measure 124.75 inches from tip to tip. That's about as long as a full-grown alligator! Texas Longhorns are admired for their horns and striking color. Most of the steers are mixed red and white in coloring. Gibralter was born on March 24, 1992, and is owned by the Dickinson Cattle Co., Inc., of Texas.

The Texas quarter features an image of the state's outline, along with a single five-point star—perfect for the "Lone Star State." A rope around the edge completes the design.

State Facts

Statehood: 12/29/1845
Rank: 28
Nickname: Lone Star State
Population: 25,145,561 (2010)
State Flower: Bluebonnet
State Bird: Mockingbird
State Tree: Pecan
State Song: "Texas, Our Texas"
Motto: *Friendship*
Postal Code: TX

Fun Facts (2009)
Amusement Parks: 55
Toy Stores: 533
Pet and Pet Supply Stores: 477

Did You Know?

Texas

- is our nation's second largest state.
- was an independent republic before statehood.
- was traveled widely by many Spanish explorers in their search for the fabled Seven Cities of Gold.
- is the location of the Alamo, perhaps the state's most important historical site.
- is where, in 1963, President John F. Kennedy was assassinated while visiting Dallas.

Complete the crossword puzzle below.

Across

3 The area south of Texas

6 The coast of Texas is on this body of water

7 A famous battle occurred here

9 Where astronauts report

10 John F. Kennedy was assassinated here

Down

1 This river is the boundary between Texas and Mexico

2 Texas Rangers Hall of Fame is here

4 You could find historical missions here

5 The Spanish built these when they claimed Texas

8 The capital of Texas

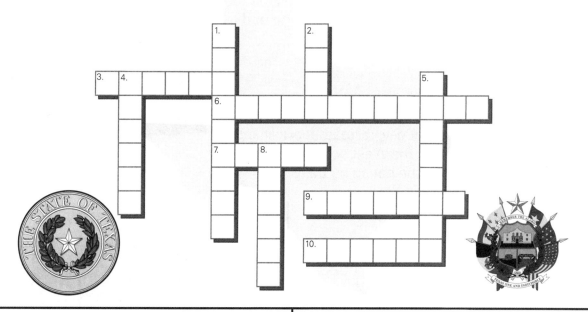

Famous Texans

- Sam Houston led the Texans against Mexico and became the first president of the Republic of Texas.
- Lieutenant Audie Murphy was the most decorated soldier in World War II.
- Dwight D. Eisenhower was the thirty-fourth president of the United States.
- Lyndon B. Johnson was the thirty-sixth president of the United States.
- Vicki Carr is a singer and a recording artist.
- Mary Martin, a singer and an actress, was the mother of actor Larry Hagman.
- Dan Rather is a national news anchor.

State Greats

- Texas, the second largest state, is 220 times larger than Rhode Island.
- About 200 Texans died defending the Alamo, a mission in San Antonio.
- The Lyndon B. Johnson Space Center in Houston is the headquarters for all manned spacecraft projects.
- The Texas Rangers Hall of Fame in Waco honors the Texas Rangers.
- The Rio Grande is the largest river in Texas and forms the boundary with Mexico.
- Texas vies with Alaska for producing the most petroleum in the United States.

Utah

Largest Slot Canyon

A slot canyon begins as a small crack in a huge rock. Over time, water and wind turn the hairline crack into a crevice large enough for people to hike through. It's not an easy hike, though. Hikers may have to climb with ropes, swim through icy water, or scramble over boulders. The Narrows slot canyon in Zion National Park, Utah, is about 2,000 feet deep. Yet, its walls are only 30 feet apart at the widest points. The Narrows snakes through Zion for 16 miles. It takes about 13 hours to get from one end to the other.

The golden spike on the Utah quarter represents an important day in 1869. On that day, railroad tracks linked the East and the West so that people could cross the nation by train.

State Facts

Utah

★ Salt Lake City

Statehood: 1/4/1896
Rank: 45
Nickname: Beehive State
Population: 2,763,885 (2010)
State Flower: Sego lily
State Bird: California seagull
State Tree: Blue spruce
State Song: "Utah, This Is the Place"
Motto: *Industry*
Postal Code: UT

Fun Facts (2009)
Amusement Parks: 5
Toy Stores: 107
Pet and Pet Supply Stores: 56

Did You Know?

Utah

- is divided in half by the spine of the Rocky Mountains.
- is the location of the Great Salt Lake, the largest salt lake in North America.
- is where, at Promontory Point in 1869, the first transcontinental railroad system in the United States was completed.
- was settled by Mormon leader Brigham Young and his band of followers.
- is a state of extremes, from hot deserts to snowcapped mountains.
- once had dinosaurs roaming its region.

Write the letter from column B next to the matching phrase in column A.

1. _____ He led Mormons to Utah.

2. _____ This lake has water you can drink.

3. _____ These people were unhappy when the Mormons came.

4. _____ Mormons originally came from here.

5. _____ This state is another part of the "Four Corners."

6. _____ You can find these kinds of bones.

A the Utes

B New York

C Brigham Young

D Colorado

E Utah Lake

F dinosaur

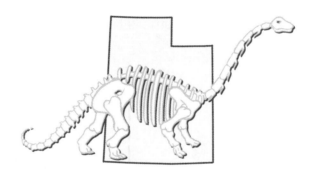

Famous Utahns

- Butch Cassidy was born George LeRoy Parker. He robbed trains and banks, giving some of the money to people in need.
- John Marriott was born near Ogden and grew up on a sheep ranch. He founded the Marriott hotel chain.
- Donny and Marie Osmond are a brother and sister team who had a hit TV show.
- Steve Young, born in Salt Lake City, won the Super Bowl with the San Francisco 49ers.
- Country singer and actress Loretta Young won an Academy Award.

State Greats

- The country's first traffic light was invented and installed in Salt Lake City in 1912.
- In 1896, Martha Hughes Cannon became the first woman to serve as a state senator. The opposing candidate was her husband.
- Lee Ann Roberts was the first woman racing driver to travel over 300 mph. She set the record on the Bonneville Salt Flats.
- Utah is one of the states that makes up the "Four Corners," where four states touch.
- So many dinosaur bones have been discovered near the Dinosaur National Monument in northeastern Utah that it is nicknamed "Dinosaurland."

Vermont

Longest Finger Knitting by a Team
June 8, 2011

On one particular wacky Wednesday at Monkton Central School in Hinesburg, Vermont, a pair of second graders saw their dream come true. They wanted to break the world record for finger knitting. Finger knitting is wrapping yarn around fingers to create a cord or a chain. The Longest Finger Knitting by a Team measured 29,812 feet long. That's 5.6 miles. The team consisted of first- and second-grade students. The students made a 45-pound yarn ball with all of the chains.

The Vermont quarter features an image of a person tapping syrup from the maple trees the state is known for. The background shows Camel's Hump Mountain.

State Facts

Statehood: 3/4/1791
Rank: 14
Nickname: Green Mountain State
Population: 625,741 (2010)
State Flower: Red clover
State Bird: Hermit thrush
State Tree: Sugar maple
State Song: "These Green Mountains"
Motto: *Freedom and Unity*
Postal Code: VT

Fun Facts (2009)
Amusement Parks: 0
Toy Stores: 22
Pet and Pet Supply Stores: 22

Did You Know?

Vermont
- is bordered on the east by the Connecticut River.
- is the only New England state without a seacoast.
- has the lowest percentage of city dwellers of any state.
- leads the nation in the production of maple syrup.
- is the birthplace of Calvin Coolidge, the thirtieth president.
- was explored by Samuel de Champlain who, in 1609, became the first European to set foot on its soil.

Use the words in the Word Bank to complete each sentence.

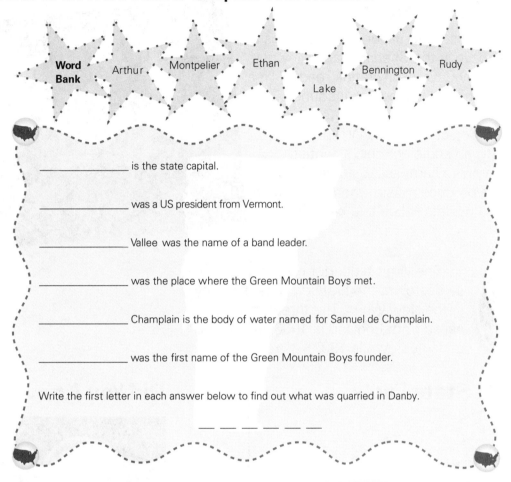

Word Bank: Arthur, Montpelier, Ethan, Lake, Bennington, Rudy

_____ is the state capital.

_____ was a US president from Vermont.

_____ Vallee was the name of a band leader.

_____ was the place where the Green Mountain Boys met.

_____ Champlain is the body of water named for Samuel de Champlain.

_____ was the first name of the Green Mountain Boys founder.

Write the first letter in each answer below to find out what was quarried in Danby.

___ ___ ___ ___ ___ ___

Famous Vermonters

- Chester A. Arthur, born in Fairfield, became the twenty-first president of the United States.
- George Dewey was a hero of the Spanish-American War and an admiral in the Navy.
- John Dewey was a philosopher and an educator.
- Stephen Douglas was a senator and ran for president against Abraham Lincoln.
- Rudy Vallee was a band leader and a singer.
- Orson Bean starred in the television show _Dr. Quinn, Medicine Woman_.
- Billy Kidd won an Olympic skiing medal in 1964.

State Greats

- Montpelier is the least populated state capital in the nation.
- Vermont was the first state to adopt a constitution that abolished slavery and gave all adult men the right to vote.
- Marble from quarries located in Danby was used in many famous buildings including the Supreme Court Building in Washington, DC.
- The granite quarries near Barre are the largest in the country.
- Burlington is the state's largest city and is called the "Queen City."

Largest Natural Underground Musical Instrument

Luray Caverns, a US national landmark, is a spectacular cave in the Shenandoah Valley of Virginia. A Luray Caverns invitation reads, "Hear Rocks Sing." This isn't as odd as it sounds. The Great Stalacpipe Organ is the result of a three-year project by Leland W. Sprinkle, a mathematician and electronic scientist. He found a way to harness 3.5 acres of stalactites to produce music when struck with rubber-tipped mallets linked to a keyboard.

The Virginia quarter honors Jamestown, the first permanent colony in the New World. The three ships sailed from England in 1606 and landed at Jamestown in 1607.

State Facts

Virginia
★ Richmond

Statehood: 6/25/1788
Rank: 10
Nickname: Old Dominion
Population: 8,001,024 (2010)
State Flower: American dogwood
State Bird: Northern cardinal
State Tree: American dogwood
State Song: "Carry Me Back to Old Virginia"
Motto: *Thus Always to Tyrants*
Postal Code: VA

Fun Facts (2009)
Amusement Parks: 11
Toy Stores: 257
Pet and Pet Supply Stores: 227

Did You Know?

Virginia
- is the location of Mount Vernon, once the home of George Washington.
- is the birthplace of eight presidents.
- is where, at Jamestown in 1607, the first permanent English settlement in North America was established.
- is where, at the town called Appomattox Court House on April 9, 1865, General Lee surrendered to General Grant, bringing an end to the Civil War.

Use the words in the Word Bank to complete the sentences.

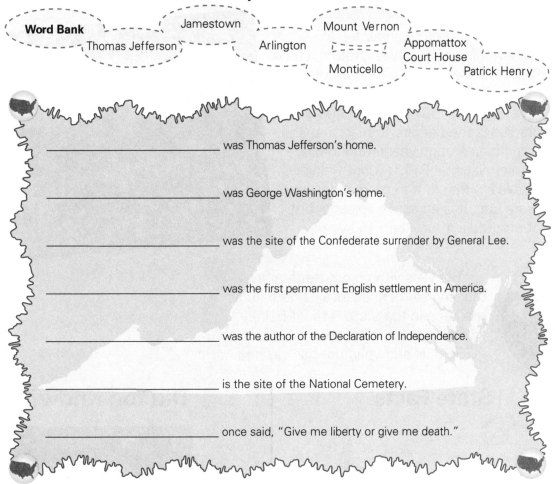

Word Bank

Jamestown

Mount Vernon

Thomas Jefferson

Arlington

Appomattox
Court House

Monticello

Patrick Henry

_____ was Thomas Jefferson's home.

_____ was George Washington's home.

_____ was the site of the Confederate surrender by General Lee.

_____ was the first permanent English settlement in America.

_____ was the author of the Declaration of Independence.

_____ is the site of the National Cemetery.

_____ once said, "Give me liberty or give me death."

Famous Virginians

- Patrick Henry was the first governor of Virginia. He once said, "Give me liberty or give me death."
- John Mercer Langston was the first African American representative to Congress from Virginia.
- Stonewall Jackson was a Confederate general during the Civil War.
- Edgar Allan Poe was famous for writing short stories and poetry.
- Meriwether Lewis and William Clark led an expedition to the Pacific Ocean.
- Richard E. Byrd was the first man to fly over the North and South Poles.

State Greats

- The surrender that ended the American Revolution took place at Yorktown.
- The surrender that ended the Civil War took place at Appomattox Court House.
- Virginia is called the "Mother of Presidents." Eight presidents were born in Virginia.
- Tobacco was once the basis of Virginia's economy.
- The Chesapeake Bay Bridge-Tunnel is the longest bridge-tunnel in the world.
- Government employment is now Virginia's number one industry.

Greatest Snowfall in 12 Months
February 18, 1972

When 1,224.5 inches of snow fell at Paradise on Mount Rainier, Washington, a new world record was set. The greatest amount of snow ever to fall in 12 months happened between February 19, 1971, and February 18, 1972. Paradise is the primary tourist stop and the only alpine area open year-round in the Mount Rainier National Park. Mount Rainier itself is a volcano that first formed about one million years ago. It is an active volcano, but it has not erupted in more than 150 years.

The Washington quarter features the king salmon, an invaluable natural resource in the state. Mount Rainier, an active volcano covered by snow and glaciers, is shown in the background.

State Facts

Washington

★Olympia

Statehood: 11/11/1889
Rank: 42
Nickname: Evergreen State
Population: 6,724,540 (2010)
State Flower: Coast rhododendron
State Bird: Willow goldfinch
State Tree: Western hemlock
State Song: "Washington, My Home"
Motto: *Bye and Bye*
Postal Code: WA

Fun Facts (2009)
Amusement Parks: 6
Toy Stores: 266
Pet and Pet Supply Stores: 263

Did You Know?

Washington
- is the location of Grand Coulee Dam, the largest concrete dam in the United States.
- is where, in 1980, the volcano Mount Saint Helens erupted.
- is the home of the Space Needle, a unique tower over 600 feet tall.
- is where, in 1962, the first municipal monorail service in the United States began operating.
- is where American fur traders built Fort Okanogan along the Columbia River.

Complete the crossword puzzle below.

Across

1. the capital city
3. an American fort
6. the name of a British explorer and a modern city
8. a famous cartoonist
9. a television pioneer

Down

2. the name of an American Indian tribe
4. the Hudson Bay Company and the Americans wanted this
5. Mount St. Helens is one, and so is Mount Rainier
7. an important forest resource

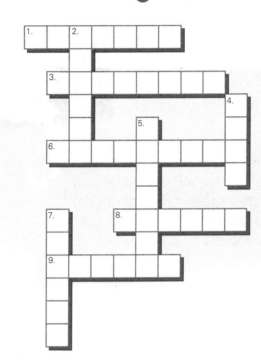

Famous Washingtonians

- Bing Crosby was a well-known singer and an actor.
- Bill Gates founded Microsoft, a computer software company.
- Edward R. Murrow was a reporter and a TV news pioneer who graduated from Washington State University.
- Richard Hugo was an award-winning poet.
- Gary Larson created "The Far Side" cartoons.
- Henry M. Jackson was an important state senator.
- Judy Collins is a singer and a songwriter.

State Greats

- The Boeing 747 airplane plant in Everett is the largest building in the United States. It covers 47 acres.
- Olympic National Park protects the North American seashore and temperate rain forest.
- Microsoft's headquarters near Seattle has made Washington a leading state in computer software technology.
- Mount Rainier has more glaciers than any other single peak in the United States. It is Washington's highest mountain.
- Trees are an important resource. Timber from Washington is shipped all over the country.

Most Eggs Held in the Hand
March 21, 2009

Here is a trick you can try at home. Take a carton of eggs out of the refrigerator. Make sure they are raw eggs and not hard-boiled eggs. How many can you hold in one hand for 10 seconds without dropping any? Four? Five? You would have to hold a lot more than that to break the record held by Zachery George of Parsons, West Virginia. He holds the record for the Most Eggs Held in the Hand, with 24.

The West Virginia quarter features an image of the New River Gorge and the bridge that spans it. The bridge is the second highest in the United States at 876 feet above the gorge.

State Facts

West Virginia

★Charleston

Statehood: 6/20/1863
Rank: 35
Nickname: Mountain State
Population: 1,852,994 (2010)
State Flower: Rhododendron
State Bird: Cardinal
State Tree: Sugar maple
State Song: "West Virginia, My Home Sweet Home"
Motto: *Mountaineers Are Always Free*
Postal Code: WV

Fun Facts (2009)
Amusement Parks: 1
Toy Stores: 37
Pet and Pet Supply Stores: 28

Did You Know?

West Virginia

- has two other state songs: "This is My West Virginia" and "The West Virginia Hills."
- was part of Virginia until the Civil War. They broke off to remain in the Union while Virginia joined the South.
- is the glass and marble manufacturing center of the United States.
- is completely covered by the Appalachian Mountains.
- is the location of Romney, a town that changed hands between the Union and the Confederacy at least 56 times during the Civil War.

Complete the sentences using facts about West Virginia.

An abolitionist named _____ _____ raided a US arsenal at Harper's Ferry.

The city of _____ was the capital before Charleston.

West Virginia's _____ is considered the best because it burns the cleanest.

_____ wanted West Virginia to rejoin it after the Civil War.

The _____ _____ forms much of West Virginia's northwestern border.

The building of the _____ created a huge demand for coal.

Famous West Virginians

- Mary Lou Retton won the gold medal in gymnastics in 1984.
- John Brown was an abolitionist who led a raid on a US arsenal at Harpers Ferry.
- Thomas "Stonewall" Jackson, born in Clarksburg, was a Confederate general who won the Battle of Bull Run against great odds. Afterward, he was accidentally killed by one of his own men.
- Chuck Yeager was the first pilot to break the sound barrier.
- Don Knotts starred in many popular TV shows.

State Greats

- West Virginia's coal is some of the best because it burns the cleanest.
- Smoke Hole Caverns are caves once used by American Indians to smoke and store meat.
- In central West Virginia, the National Radio Astronomy Observatory has some of the world's largest radio telescopes.
- White Sulphur Springs is a mineral spring health spa where several presidents have vacationed.
- The Blenko Glass Company in Milton made the windows of the National Cathedral in Washington, DC, and the Cathedral of St. John the Divine in New York City.

Wisconsin

Largest Cheese Sculpture
August 14, 2011

Wisconsin is home to more than 120 cheese factories. It's no wonder that so many people think "cheese" when they think "Wisconsin." This is just fine with artist Sarah Kaufmann, otherwise known as "the Cheese Lady." Kaufmann carved a cheddar cheese sculpture that weighed 925 pounds at the 160th anniversary of the Wisconsin State Fair in West Allis, Wisconsin. It took Kaufmann a total of 36 hours to complete the sculpture. To illustrate state fair fun, the sculpture included a pig, a cow, a boy, a sprite, and a chicken riding on a roller coaster.

The Wisconsin quarter highlights the state's pride in its dairy products and agriculture: a cow, a wheel of cheese, and an ear of corn. More than one million cows live in Wisconsin!

State Facts

Wisconsin

Madison ★

Statehood: 5/29/1848
Rank: 30
Nicknames: Badger State, America's Dairyland
Population: 5,686,986 (2010)
State Flower: Wood violet
State Bird: Robin
State Tree: Sugar maple
State Song: "On Wisconsin!"
Motto: *Forward*
Postal Code: WI

Fun Facts (2009)
Amusement Parks: 8
Toy Stores: 191
Pet and Pet Supply Stores: 162

Did You Know?

Wisconsin
- is named for an Ojibwa word meaning "gathering of the waters."
- leads the nation in the production of milk and cheese.
- is where, at Green Bay in 1634, Jean Nicolet, a French explorer, became the first European to set foot on its soil.
- is where, at Racine in 1887, malted milk was created by William Horlick.
- was originally home to the Winnebago, Dakota, and Menominee tribes; and later the Sauk Fox, Kickapoo, and Potawatomi tribes.

Complete the crossword puzzle below.

Across

2 not a "great" lake

5 visit this city near Lake Michigan

6 a nickname for Wisconsinites

7 not just a city, a body of water, too

Down

1 it's the only Great Lake entirely in the United States

3 this city has a different colored bay

4 an inland city

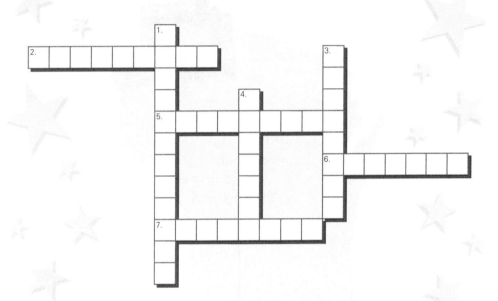

Famous Wisconsinites

- Gene Wilder was born Jerome (Jerry) Silberman and is an actor.
- Vince Lombardi coached the Green Bay Packers to victory in the first two Super Bowls. The Super Bowl trophy is named after him.
- Wladziu Valentino Liberace was a flashy classical pianist known commonly by his last name.
- Joseph McCarthy was a US senator who investigated people whom he suspected of being unpatriotic communists.
- Oshkosh was a Menominee who lobbied the federal government to grant his people a reservation. The city of Oshkosh is named after him.

State Greats

- Facial tissues were invented by a Wisconsin paper company in 1917.
- Wisconsin produces a lot of milk. In fact, it produces enough to fill 11 Olympic-sized swimming pools a day.
- Wisconsinites were given the nickname "badgers" because early lead miners dug shelters underground.
- On October 8, 1871, the same night of the famous Chicago fires, a fire swept through Peshtigo, killing about 1,200 people.
- The first kindergarten in the United States was set up in Watertown in 1856.

Wyoming

Oldest National Park
1872

Imagine a place where buffalo roam freely, where hot springs and mud pots bubble and boil, and where geysers shoot high into the air. This place is Yellowstone National Park. Yellowstone was the first area in the world to be named a national park. In 1872, US President Ulysses S. Grant declared that Yellowstone would always be a special place "for the benefit and enjoyment of the people." The park stretches across 3,470 square miles, mostly in the state of Wyoming.

The bucking horse and rider on the Wyoming quarter represent the state's Wild West heritage. It was nicknamed the "Equality State," as it was the first state to grant women the right to vote.

State Facts

Wyoming

Cheyenne ★

Statehood: 7/10/1890
Rank: 44
Nickname: Equality State
Population: 563,626 (2010)
State Flower: Indian paintbrush
State Bird: Meadowlark
State Tree: Cottonwood
State Song: "Wyoming"
Motto: *Equal Rights*
Postal Code: WY

Fun Facts (2009)
Amusement Parks: 0
Toy Stores: 17
Pet and Pet Supply Stores: 22

Did You Know?

Wyoming
- is also known as the "Cowboy State."
- is the least populated of all the states.
- is the location of Devils Tower, set aside by Congress in 1906 as the nation's first national monument.
- is the location of Old Faithful, the most famous geyser in the United States.
- became, in 1869, the first state in the nation to grant women the right to vote.
- became, with the election of Nellie Tayloe Ross in 1924, the first state to choose a woman as its governor.

Use these clues to find words about Wyoming in the word search below.

★ the first National Park
★ the capital of Wyoming
★ the name of an artist

★ the state nickname
★ these mountains are "grand"
★ a woman was elected to this position in 1924

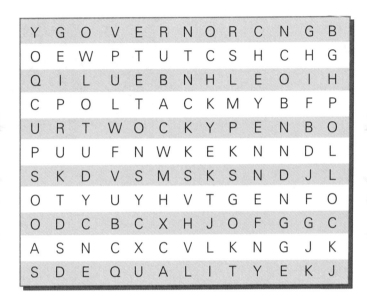

Y	G	O	V	E	R	N	O	R	C	N	G	B
O	E	W	P	T	U	T	C	S	H	C	H	G
Q	I	L	U	E	B	N	H	L	E	O	I	H
C	P	O	L	T	A	C	K	M	Y	B	F	P
U	R	T	W	O	C	K	Y	P	E	N	B	O
P	U	U	F	N	W	K	E	K	N	N	D	L
S	K	D	V	S	M	S	K	S	N	D	J	L
O	T	Y	U	Y	H	V	T	G	E	N	F	O
O	D	C	B	C	X	H	J	O	F	G	G	C
A	S	N	C	X	C	V	L	K	N	G	J	K
S	D	E	Q	U	A	L	I	T	Y	E	K	J

Famous Wyomingites

- Jackson Pollock, born near Cody, was an artist.
- Joe Alexander was a world champion rodeo star.
- Curt Gowdy was a sportscaster whose television show, *The American Sportsman*, ran for about 20 years.
- Nancy Curtis started a book publishing company, High Plains Press, in 1984 and still runs it from her cattle ranch.
- In 1870, Esther Hobart Morris became the first female judge in the United States.
- Patricia MacLachlan won the Newbery Medal for her children's book *Sarah, Plain and Tall*.

State Greats

- Old Faithful is the most famous geyser in the United States.
- Yellowstone National Park was established in 1872.
- About two tons of coal per second are dug at Black Thunder, the biggest coal mine in the Americas.
- Wyoming elected the nation's first female governor, Nellie Tayloe Ross, in 1924.
- There are fewer people in Wyoming than in any other state.
- Wyoming has about a half-million residents, but more than 5 million tourists come to visit every year.

Most People to Do Jumping Jacks in 24 Hours
October 11–12, 2011

First Lady Michelle Obama and 464 children practiced jumping jacks for one minute on the lawn of the White House in Washington, DC. The event was part of the first lady's "Let's Move" plan to fight childhood obesity. During this 24-hour record-breaking event, a total of 300,265 people performed jumping jacks at 1,050 locations around the world. The record attempt was called "Let's Jump!" and was organized by *National Geographic Kids*.

In 2009, The United States Mint created quarters for the District of Columbia and five US territories. This quarter features an image of musician Edward Kennedy "Duke" Ellington.

State Facts

Washington, DC, is not a state. It is the District of Columbia and capital of the United States of America. Its area is 68 square miles.

Population: 601,723 (2010)
Flower: American beauty rose
Bird: Wood thrush
Tree: Scarlet oak
Song: "The Star-Spangled Banner"
Motto: *Justice for All*
Postal Code: DC

Fun Facts (2009)
Amusement Parks: 0
Toy Stores: 6
Pet and Pet Supply Stores: 10

Did You Know?

Washington, DC
- was created by Congress so that the capital of the United States would not belong to any one state.
- was planned to hold the Capitol building and the President's House, later called the White House.
- was originally named District of Columbia, or "DC." It was renamed Washington in honor of George Washington.
- was mostly burned to the ground in the War of 1812 by British forces.

Andrew wants to work for the FBI one day. He wants to use codes to protect government secrets. This is Andrew's list of the best things to see in DC. Use his code to find out what he likes best about DC.

What to see in DC:

the tall, 555-foot tower
_____ _____

the road that connects the Capitol and the White House
_____ _____

the monument honoring Lincoln
_____ _____

the rectangular body of water
_____ _____

To find Andrew's favorite area of the city, follow these decoding steps.

1 Write the first letter of each word in each answer on the line. _____

2 Cross out the W, M, P, R, and P. Write the remaining letters on the line. _____

3 Rewrite the remaining letters on the line. Add an L. _____

4 Unscramble the letters to find Andrew's favorite place in DC. _____

Famous Washingtonians

- Edward Albee won three Pulitzer Prizes for his plays.
- Duke Ellington was a famous jazz and blues musician.
- John Foster Dulles was a secretary of state.
- Edward Brooke was the first African American senator elected by popular vote.
- J. Edgar Hoover directed the Federal Bureau of Investigation.
- John Philip Sousa was a bandmaster and a composer who was famous for his marches.

Capital Greats

- The Mall is a grassy area between the Capitol and the Potomac River. Most of the national museums and many of the monuments are on the Mall.
- The Washington Monument is a hollow tower that stands about 555 feet and 6 inches tall.
- The Lincoln Memorial contains a large statue of President Lincoln created by Daniel French.
- George Washington University is a leading university in DC.
- The Theodore Roosevelt Memorial is located on an island in the Potomac River.

When you mail something to someone, the state in the address is always abbreviated using two letters. See how many postal abbreviations you know!

_____ Alabama	_____ Louisiana	_____ North Dakota
_____ Alaska	_____ Maine	_____ Ohio
_____ Arizona	_____ Maryland	_____ Oklahoma
_____ Arkansas	_____ Massachusetts	_____ Oregon
_____ California	_____ Michigan	_____ Pennsylvania
_____ Colorado	_____ Minnesota	_____ Rhode Island
_____ Connecticut	_____ Mississippi	_____ South Carolina
_____ Delaware	_____ Missouri	_____ South Dakota
_____ Florida	_____ Montana	_____ Tennessee
_____ Georgia	_____ Nebraska	_____ Texas
_____ Hawaii	_____ Nevada	_____ Utah
_____ Idaho	_____ New Hampshire	_____ Vermont
_____ Illinois	_____ New Jersey	_____ Virginia
_____ Indiana	_____ New Mexico	_____ Washington
_____ Iowa	_____ New York	_____ West Virginia
_____ Kansas	_____ North Carolina	_____ Wisconsin
_____ Kentucky		_____ Wyoming

United States Word Search

Find each state name and the District of Columbia in this puzzle.

```
N A M V M A F D E E Q Q M W E S T V I R G I N I A
O S R O E A L O C J H V J W M I S S I S S I P P I
R O D I N R I A K W Q G K Y R H O D E I S L A N D
T U N I Z T M N C A L I F O R N I A S T P S Q B T
H T E P S O A O E W A S H I N G T O N K J N M C N
C H W E C T N N L O U I S I A N A A Z I K S S U
A C H N O N R A A T N E W M E X I C O H X O Q J O
R A A N N O A I T U J B K D N E W J E R S E Y I B
O R M S N R W P C B N Z O M I S S O U R I F H V G
L O P Y E T A Z T T V G V R O L B I M R P O A N M
I L S L C H I X E A O O E Z E J Q C L W C D I E A
N I H V T D I N N R O F L O U G F O U O A M A M H
A N I A I A E R N K H O C J R D O F J V O N A S C
M A R N C K B Y E A K G V O P G Z N E Y A B T S M
Q I E I U O S Q S N E W R B L T I N W I A T I J A
G L V A T T O M S S N F E H P U O A D L E U B Q R
Y L F O V A U I E A T F Q S H H M N A S I Z O Y Y
C I M K I L T N E S U O D D A I I B U A H O S L L
O N I L R U H N F H C S M D I K A H I K L U W L A
L O C A G M D E V I K Y I A R D C H W A A A T A N
O I H H I U A S G Z Y S W O I A G L I R R N S A D
R S I O N P K O Z G A A Y R S I M D W T P X S K H
A F G M I Z O T H X H W O S N E B R A S K A I A A
D C A A A L T A E L E L A T E S D E L A W A R E S
O I N Y A O A T A N F M W I S C O N S I N L F L O
```

In the top 12 horizontal rows, circle the first unused letter. The unused letters, in order, will complete the sentence below.

___ ___ ___ ___ ___ ___ **and** ___ ___ ___ ___ ___ ___

are NOT part of the *contiguous* (sharing a common boundary) United States.

See if you can solve the crossword puzzle on page 113 using the clues below. Hint: All answers are state names.

Across

4. You can eat lots of lobster in this state. Its only bordering state is New Hampshire.
5. The largest concrete dam in the United States is here. Water is one of this state's most important resources.
7. Brigham Young loved this state.
10. This state consists of a group of 132 islands formed from volcanic mountains.
11. This state is the Heart of Dixie.
13. This gem of a state produces a lot of silver and lead.
14. This big state contains the cattle capital and the Manned Space Flight Center.
15. The "Sooner" you visit this state, the better.
16. The world's highest suspension bridge for vehicles can be found in this "high" state.

Down

1. A history of Mexican and American Indian influence is evident in this warm, dry state.
2. This state is a leading producer of peaches, peanuts, and tobacco.
3. In the Hawkeye State, much corn, soybeans, beef cattle, hogs, and dairy products are produced.
4. This state was the sixth state to join the Union and is the sixth smallest in size.
6. First in size but second to last in population accurately describes this state.
8. This state has the largest population, the highest agriculture output, and the tallest and oldest living things.
9. The Chesapeake Bay separates this state into two parts.
12. Although Lewis and Clark explored this state in 1805, it was the discovery of gold that brought the first settlers to this "treasure" state.

Riddles are so much fun to try to solve! Read the riddles. Then, decide which state solves each riddle.

1 I am a "gem" of a state. My potatoes are found all over the United States. Hells Canyon and Shoshone Falls can be visited in me. Which state am I? _____

2 Montgomery is my capital. I was once a one-crop (cotton) state. My state flower is the camellia. Which state am I? _____

3 Less rain falls in me than in any other state. I am home to the Hoover Dam and Carson City. I'm not gold, but I am silver. Which state am I? _____

4 I was the first state to secede from the Union. My Fort Sumter was the place where the Civil War began. I am the Palmetto State. Which state am I? _____

5 My Jamestown was the site of the first permanent English settlement in America. Patrick Henry gave his famous speech in my Appomattox Court House. Which state am I? _____

6 I am the 42nd state. The Cascade Mountains divide me. The Grand Coulee Dam can be found in me. Which state am I? _____

7 I am the "Land of Lincoln." I contain one of the world's busiest airports. I am a leader in soybean and corn production. Which state am I? _____

8 My people are "Hoosiers." I am the 19th state. The University of Notre Dame is located in me. Which state am I? _____

9 I am the Old Line State. I'm separated into two parts by the Chesapeake Bay. Annapolis is my capital. Which state am I? _____

10 I was born during the Civil War as a result of the Civil War. Charleston is my capital. The site of John Brown's raid is in me. Which state am I? _____

11 My name means "mountainous." I'm a real "treasure." Many of the mountains in my Glacier National Park have never been climbed. Which state am I?

_____

12 Gerald Ford was born in me. I contain the only national forest planted by foresters. Lincoln is my capital. Which state am I? _____

13 My name means "swift wind." I am located in the center of the original 48 states. You can see sunflowers growing in me. Which state am I? _____

14 Abraham Lincoln was born in me. A famous derby is held in me. The nation's gold vault is in my Fort Knox. Which state am I? _____

15 You can find lots of "sunshine" in me. My Saint Augustine is the oldest city in the United States. Rockets launch out of my Kennedy Space Center. Which state am I?

_____

16 I lead the nation in tobacco farming. Wooden furniture and cloth are important products in my economy. Which state am I? _____

17 I am big—220 times the size of Rhode Island! I have the most farms, farmland, cattle, horses, and sheep in the nation. Which state am I? _____

18 I believe in "equality." My capital and largest city has only about 50,000 people. Half of my land is federally owned and operated. Which state am I? _____

19 I am the highest state in the nation. The highest road in the United States is in me. The Rocky Mountains are a big part of me. Which state am I? _____

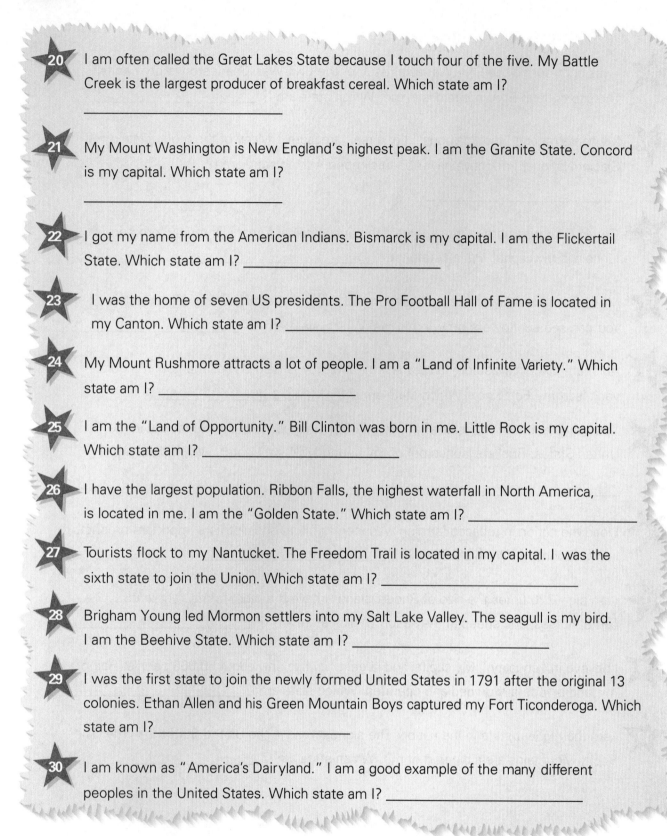

20 I am often called the Great Lakes State because I touch four of the five. My Battle Creek is the largest producer of breakfast cereal. Which state am I?

_____

21 My Mount Washington is New England's highest peak. I am the Granite State. Concord is my capital. Which state am I?

_____

22 I got my name from the American Indians. Bismarck is my capital. I am the Flickertail State. Which state am I? _____

23 I was the home of seven US presidents. The Pro Football Hall of Fame is located in my Canton. Which state am I? _____

24 My Mount Rushmore attracts a lot of people. I am a "Land of Infinite Variety." Which state am I? _____

25 I am the "Land of Opportunity." Bill Clinton was born in me. Little Rock is my capital. Which state am I? _____

26 I have the largest population. Ribbon Falls, the highest waterfall in North America, is located in me. I am the "Golden State." Which state am I? _____

27 Tourists flock to my Nantucket. The Freedom Trail is located in my capital. I was the sixth state to join the Union. Which state am I? _____

28 Brigham Young led Mormon settlers into my Salt Lake Valley. The seagull is my bird. I am the Beehive State. Which state am I? _____

29 I was the first state to join the newly formed United States in 1791 after the original 13 colonies. Ethan Allen and his Green Mountain Boys captured my Fort Ticonderoga. Which state am I? _____

30 I am known as "America's Dairyland." I am a good example of the many different peoples in the United States. Which state am I? _____

31 I am the biggest state. The highest peak in the United States, Mount McKinley, is located in me. Which state am I? _____

32 I contain the Grand Canyon. Phoenix is my capital. Without irrigation, half of me would be desert. Which state am I? _____

33 I am the Garden State. My Atlantic City offers lots of exciting things for visitors to do. The violet is my flower. Which state am I? _____

34 I am the First State. I was named for Lord De La Warr. I was the first state to ratify the new constitution in 1787. Which state am I? _____

35 I am the first state in the United States to greet the sun each day. I lead the nation with my lobster catch. Ninety percent of my land is covered by woods. Which state am I?

_____

36 In 1610, I was founded by the Spanish. I am the "Land of Enchantment." My Santa Fe is the oldest seat of government in the nation. Which state am I?

_____

37 My Hartford is known as "Insurance City." The first constitution in the New World was adopted in me in 1639. Which state am I? _____

38 I can "show" you a lot. Jefferson City is my capital. In the summer of 1993, much of my land flooded. Which state am I? _____

39 I lead the nation in banking and wholesale trade. I contain the nation's largest city. I am the Empire State. Which state am I? _____

40 I am "the land where the corn grows tall." Des Moines is my capital. Which state am I?

_____

⭐ **41** Portland is my largest city. My Columbia River Gorge attracts many tourists. There is year-round skiing at my Mount Hood. Which state am I? _____

⭐ **42** I am the Gopher State. My Mesabi Range contains much iron ore. St. Paul is my capital. Which state am I? _____

⭐ **43** I am the tiniest state. Roger Williams founded me in 1636. I produce the most costume jewelry in the world. Which state am I? _____

⭐ **44** My name is an American Indian word meaning "red people." The Five Civilized Tribes wanted me to become the state of Sequoyah in 1905. Instead, I am the Sooner State. Which state am I? _____

⭐ **45** La Salle claimed my area for France in 1682. The US bought me from France in 1803. I am the 18th state. Which state am I? _____

⭐ **46** Elvis Presley was born in my Tupelo. I am the Magnolia State. Jackson is my capital and largest city. Which state am I? _____

⭐ **47** You probably love my peaches. My most famous peanut farmer is Jimmy Carter. I am the Empire State of the South. Which state am I? _____

⭐ **48** I was the second state to ratify the Constitution. I was the center, or "keystone," of the original 13 colonies. Which state am I? _____

⭐ **49** I am the 50th state. My Pearl Harbor is very famous. Diamond Head is one of my most famous extinct volcanoes. Which state am I? _____

⭐ **50** I have an east, a middle, and a west. My state capital is the home of country music. I am the Volunteer State. Which state am I? _____

The United States borders more water than land. The oceans and countries around its borders have helped shape its culture. Use a map of the United States to answer the following questions. Write the state abbreviations as your answers.

1. List the states that share a border with Canada: _____

    _____

    List the states that share a border with Mexico: _____

    _____

    List the states that share a border with Russia: _____

    _____

2. List the states that touch the Arctic Ocean: _____

    List the states that touch the Pacific Ocean: _____

    _____

    List the states that touch the Atlantic Ocean, including the Gulf of Mexico: _____

    _____

    _____

    Of the states on the Atlantic Ocean, how many border the Gulf of Mexico? _____

3. List the states that touch any of the Great Lakes (Lake Superior, Lake Michigan, Lake

    Huron, Lake Erie, Lake Ontario): _____

    _____

4. List the states that touch the Mississippi River: _____

    _____

5. List the states that share a border with Missouri: _____

    _____

    List the states that share a border with Massachusetts: _____

    List the states that share a border with Mississippi: _____

    List the states that share a border with Oregon: _____

    List the states that share a border with South Dakota: _____

    _____

6. List the states that share a border with the nation's capital: _____

Temperature Trends

Use the chart to answer the following questions.

	Northern States			Central States			Southern States		
	Washington	Minnesota	Maine	California	Nebraska	Virginia	Arizona	Texas	Florida
Average Temperature in January (Fahrenheit)	30°	08°	15°	44°	23°	36°	41°	46°	59°
Average Temperature in July (Fahrenheit)	66°	70°	67°	75°	76°	75°	80°	83°	81°

1. In January, how much warmer is it in Florida than in Minnesota? _____°F

2. In July, how much cooler is it in Maine than in Arizona? _____°F

3. In California, how much warmer is it in July than it is in January? _____°F

4. In Virginia, how much cooler is it in January than it is in July? _____°F

5. Which central state has the coldest January temperature? _____

   Which central state has the warmest July temperature? _____

6. Which state has the warmest average temperature in January?_____

   Which state has the warmest average temperature in July? _____

   What region(s) are these states in? _____

7. Which state has the coolest average temperature in January? _____

   Which state has the coolest average temperature in July? _____

   What region(s) are these states in? _____

8. Which state has the least temperature change between January and July?

   _____

   What is this temperature change? _____°F

   What region is this state in? _____

9. Which state has the greatest temperature change between January and July?

   _____

   What is this temperature change? _____°F

   What region is this state in?_____

10. What conclusions can you draw from the answers to questions 6 and 8, and 7 and 9?

   _____

   _____

Let's go on a road trip! It is always fun to decipher the sayings written on some cars' license plates. Read each license plate below and write its meaning on the line beneath it.

1.

_____

2.

_____

3.

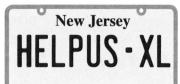

_____

4.

_____

5.

_____

6.

_____

7.

_____

8.

_____

9.

_____

State Abbreviations Word Fun

All state names can be written as two-letter abbreviations or postal codes. Combine the postal codes for each pair of states to come up with a new word.

1. California + Maine = _____ 2. Louisiana + Maine = _____

3. Oregon + California = _____ 4. Virginia + Nebraska = _____

5. Wisconsin + Delaware = _____ 6. Massachusetts + Nebraska = _____

7. Michigan + Maine = _____ 8. Hawaii + Delaware = _____

9. Delaware + Arkansas = _____ 10. Pennsylvania + Idaho = _____

11. Washington + Nebraska = _____ 12. Missouri + Oregon = _____

13. Indiana + Kentucky = _____ 14. Rhode Island + Delaware = _____

15. Pennsylvania + Indiana = _____ 16. Michigan + California = _____

17. Georgia + Maine = _____ 18. Colorado + Delaware = _____

19. Pennsylvania + Illinois = _____ 20. Colorado + Indiana = _____

21. Delaware + Alabama = _____ 22. Indiana + California = _____

23. Louisiana + North Dakota = _____ 24. Oregon + Alabama = _____

25. Washington + Illinois = _____ 26. Colorado + Alabama = _____

27. Nebraska + Arkansas = _____ 28. Michigan + North Dakota = _____

29. Massachusetts + Indiana = _____ 30. California + Nebraska = _____

31. Pennsylvania + Nebraska = _____ 32. Maine + Alabama = _____

33. Missouri + Delaware = _____ 34. Louisiana + Nebraska = _____

BONUS: Combine the postal codes for each set of three states to make a new word.

35. Florida + Oregon + Alabama = _____

36. California + North Dakota + Oregon = _____

Write the name of your home state on the curved line near the top of the quarter. Then, draw a famous person, place, or thing that you can proudly say is from your state. Above *E PLURIBUS UNUM*, write what year it is today.

E PLURIBUS UNUM

1. _____ It features the famous Gateway Arch in St. Louis.

2. _____ It shows two bison grazing in the Badlands.

3. _____ Its design includes a race car.

4. _____ It features King Kamehameha I.

5. _____ It shows "Lady Liberty."

6. _____ It shows the state's outline surrounded by the Great Lakes.

7. _____ It shows an image of a peach.

8. _____ It shows a pioneer family traveling in a covered wagon.

9. _____ It features the state tree and its flower, the magnolia.

10. _____ It features a horse in front of a mansion.

11. _____ It shows a trumpet to symbolizes the birth of jazz.

12. _____ It shows a bucking horse and a rider.

13. _____ It features a person tapping syrup from a maple tree.

14. _____ It celebrates the courage of Helen Keller.

15. _____ It shows George Washington crossing the Delaware River.

16. _____ It is marked with 21 stars because the state's rank is 21.

17. _____ It features the state's famous Charter Oak tree.

18. _____ It shows a loon floating on a lake.

19. _____ It shows a bear catching a salmon.

20. _____ It features the lighthouse at Pemaquid Point.

Page 9

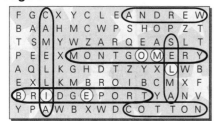

Mobile

Page 11

Page 13

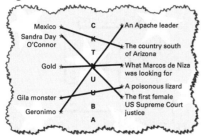

TUBAC

Page 15

BILL; BUFFALO; LA SALLE; TONTI; HOPE; MAYA; ARKANSAS POST

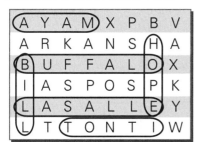

Page 17

POPPY; WHITNEY; DEATH VALLEY; YOSEMITE; MISSIONS; HOLLYWOOD; GOLDEN

Page 19

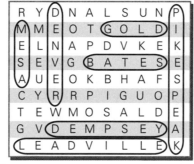

Page 21

Page 23

FIRST; DOVER; MARYLAND; ALLEN; RODNEY

Page 25

Everglades; orange blossom; fountain; Okeechobee; capital; Augustine

Page 27

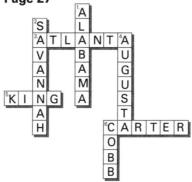

Page 29

Page 31

Lewis; Clark; Idaho; Sacajawea; Borglum

Page 33

Lincoln; Black Hawk; Michigan; Rockford; Ferris; Cardinal

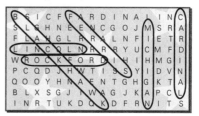

Page 35

ABRAHAM; STUDEBAKER; COLTS; TECUMSEH

Page 37

POPCORN; SCHICK; MAYTAG; DUBUQUE; RIVERSIDE; DES MOINES

Page 39

TO THE STARS THROUGH DIFFICULTIES; Sample answer: "Keep trying" or "Never be afraid to try for your goals, even if it is hard."; Answers will vary.

Page 41

LINCOLN; DANIEL BOONE; LOUISVILLE; BOWLING GREEN; FRANKFORT; UNITED WE STAND, DIVIDED WE FALL

Page 43

Satchmo; Capote; magnolia; Zydeco; pelican; Caddo; La Salle

Page 45

BANGOR; AUGUSTA; PULITZER; PINE; HAMLIN; LOBSTER

Page 47

C; B; F; D; E; A

Page 49

D; C; E; B; A; F

Page 51

GERALD; EDISON; PONTIAC; DETROIT; LAKE ERIE; LANSING

Page 53

SUPERIOR; HUBERT; SNELLING; ATLANTIC; ST. PAUL; OJIBWA

Page 55
F; F; T; F; T; F; T

Page 57
CARSON; TRUMAN; CARVER; HANNIBAL; MAINE; BAGNELL

Page 59
STEVENSVILLE; UREY; GOLD; PICTOGRAPH; BUFFALO

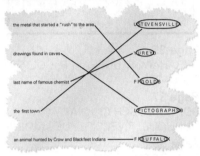

Page 61
T; F; T; F; T; T; F

Page 63
LAS VEGAS; THE SILVER STATE; WADDIE MITCHELL; HOOVER DAM; ADAVEN

Page 65

Page 67

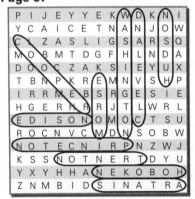

Page 69
ALBUQUERQUE; SANTA FE; O'KEEFFE; THE RIO GRANDE; ASOT; TAOS

Page 71
WOODY; HUDSON; GIOVANNI; ALBANY; ROCHESTER; HIAWATHA

Page 73
MADISON; WRIGHT; MONK; JORDAN; REVELS; LOST COLONY

Page 75

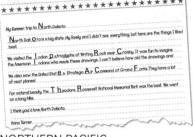

NORTHERN PACIFIC

Page 77
F; T; F; F; T; T

Page 79
OKLAHOMA CITY; BARITE ROSE; CHICKASAW; CORONADO; TRAIL OF TEARS

Page 81
CLATSOP; CLEARY; NEZ PERCE; GRAY; NOBEL; KNIGHT

Page 83
IROQUOIS; KING CHARLES; PONTIAC; COSBY; QUAKERS

Page 85
1. E; 2. C; 3. A; 4. B; 5. D

Page 87
CHARLESTON; MYRTLE BEACH; GEORGIA; FORT SUMTER; HILTON HEAD ISLAND; COLUMBIA

Page 89

Page 91
1. SMOKY MOUNTAINS;
2. SEQUOYAH; 3. ELVIS PRESLEY;
4. ALEX HALEY; 5. ALVIN YORK;
6. TANASI; 7. FRANKLIN; 8. JAMES POLK; 9. DAVY CROCKETT; NASHVILLE

Page 93

Page 95
1. C; 2. E; 3. A; 4. B; 5. D; 6. F

Page 97
Montpelier; Arthur; Rudy; Bennington; Lake; Ethan; MARBLE

Page 99
Monticello; Mount Vernon; Appomattox; Jamestown; Thomas Jefferson; Arlington; Patrick Henry

Page 101

Page 103
John Brown; Wheeling; coal; Virginia; Ohio River; railroad

Page 105

Page 107

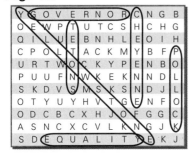

Page 109

Washington Monument; Pennsylvania Avenue; Lincoln Memorial; Reflecting Pool; MALL

Page 110

AL; AK; AZ; AR; CA; CO; CT; DE; FL; GA; HI; ID; IL; IN; IA; KS; KY; LA; ME; MD; MA; MI; MN; MS; MO; MT; NE; NV; NH; NJ; NM; NY; NC; ND; OH; OK; OR; PA; RI; SC; SD; TN; TX; UT; VT; VA; WA; WV; WI; WY

Page 111

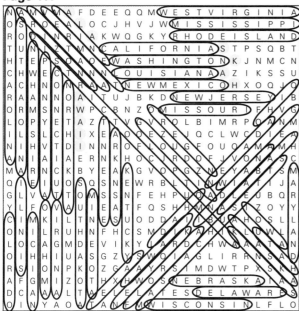

Alaska and Hawaii

Page 113

Page 114

Idaho; Alabama; Nevada; South Carolina; Virginia; Washington; Illinois; Indiana; Maryland

Page 115

West Virginia; Montana; Nebraska; Kansas; Kentucky; Florida; North Carolina; Texas; Wyoming; Colorado

Page 116

Michigan; New Hampshire; North Dakota; Ohio; South Dakota; Arkansas; California; Massachusetts; Utah; Vermont; Wisconsin

Page 117

Alaska; Arizona; New Jersey; Delaware; Maine; New Mexico; Connecticut; Missouri; New York; Iowa

Page 118

Oregon; Minnesota; Rhode Island; Oklahoma; Louisiana; Mississippi; Georgia; Pennsylvania; Hawaii; Tennessee

Page 119

1. Canada: ME, NH, VT, NY, MI, MN, ND, MT, ID, WA, AK, Mexico, TX, NM, AZ, CA; Russia: no states; 2. Arctic: AK; Pacific: AK, HI, WA, OR, CA; Atlantic: TX, LA, MS, AL, FL, GA, SC, NC, VA, DE, MD, NJ, NY, CT, MA, RI, NH, ME; Border Gulf: 5; 3. Great Lakes: NY, PA, OH, IN, IL, MI, WI, MN; 4. Mississippi River: MN, WI, IA, IL, MO, KY, TN, AR, MS, LA; 5. Missouri: IA, IL, KY, TN, AR, OK, KS; Massachusetts: VT, NH, NY, CT, RI; Mississippi: TN, AL, LA, AR, Oregon: WA, ID, NV, CA; South Dakota: ND, MN, IA, NE, WY, MT; 6. Nation's Capital: MD, VA

Page 120

1. 51°F; 2. 13°F; 3. 31°F; 4. 39°F; 5. Nebraska, Nebraska; 6. Florida, Texas, southern; 7. Minnesota, Washington, northern; 8. Florida, 22°, southern; 9. Minnesota, 62°, northern; 10. Southern states are warmer, and there is less variation in temperature between seasons. Northern states are cooler, and there is more variation in temperature between seasons.

Page 121

1. Hate to be late; 2. love animals;
3. Help us excel; 4. laughing out loud at you; 5. Rescue me; 6. You are a cutie;
7. Wait for me; 8. Excuse me;
9. guitar guy

Page 122

1. came; 2. lame; 3. orca; 4. vane;
5. wide; 6. mane; 7. mime; 8. hide;
9. dear; 10. paid; 11. wane; 12. moor;
13. inky; 14. ride; 15. pain; 16. mica;
17. game; 18. code; 19. pail; 20. coin;
21. deal; 22. Inca; 23. land; 24. oral;
25. wail; 26. coal; 27. near; 28. mind;
29. main; 30. cane; 31. pane; 32. meal;
33. mode; 34. lane; 35. floral;
36. candor

Page 123

Answers will vary. Accept all designs that contain the state name, the year, and an appropriate design.

Page 124

1. Missouri; 2. North Dakota;
3. Indiana; 4. Hawaii; 5. New York;
6. Michigan; 7. Georgia; 8. Nebraska;
9. Mississippi; 10. Kentucky;
11. Louisiana; 12. Wyoming;
13. Vermont; 14. Alabama;
15. New Jersey; 16. Illinois;
17. Connecticut; 18. Minnesota;
19. Alaska; 20. Maine

Photo Credits

Alabama: Ranald Mackechnie/Guinness World Records; Alaska: Image Copyright Sirko Hartmann, 2012, Used Under License From Shutterstock.com; Arizona: NOAO/AURA/NSF; Arkansas: John Cancalosi/naturepl.com; California: Drew Gardner/Guinness World Records; Colorado: Guinness World Records; Connecticut: Barbara Alper/Guinness World Records; Delaware: © 2008 Speakman Company; Florida: Image Copyright Loic Giraud, 2012, Used Under License From Shutterstock.com; Georgia: Dave Santucci/Guinness World Records; Hawaii: Guinness World Records; Idaho: Guinness World Records; Illinois: Ranald Mackechnie/Guinness World Records; Indiana: Guinness World Records; Iowa: Guinness World Records; Kansas: Focus On Sport/Getty Images; Kentucky: Guinness World Records; Louisiana: Guinness World Records; Maine: Guinness World Records; Maryland: Guinness World Records; Massachusetts: Guinness World Records; Michigan: Ranald Mackechnie/ Guinness World Records; Minnesota: Guinness World Records; Mississippi: © 2007 Mississippi Institute of Aesthetics, Nails, & Cosmetology; Missouri: Guinness World Records; Montana: © 2003 Dynamic Graphics, Inc.; Nebraska: Courtesy of NOAA; Nevada: Guinness World Records; New Hampshire: Guinness World Records; New Jersey: Richard Bradbury/Guinness World Records; New Mexico: Ranald Mackechnie/Guinness World Records; New York: Guinness World Records; North Carolina: Guinness World Records; North Dakota: Guinness World Records; Ohio: Guinness World Records; Oklahoma: Scott Miller/Guinness World Records; Oregon: © 2012 Steven Saubert; Pennsylvania: Guinness World Records; Rhode Island: Guinness World Records; South Carolina: Guinness World Records; South Dakota: Guinness World Records; Tennessee: Guinness World Records; Texas: Photo Courtesy of Dickinson Cattle Co., Inc.; Utah: Image Copyright Tom Grundy, 2012, Used Under License From Shutterstock.com; Vermont: Guinness World Records; Virginia: © Luray Caverns, Luray, VA; Washington: © 1999 PhotoDisc, Inc.; West Virginia: Guinness World Records; Wisconsin: Guinness World Records; Wyoming: © 2013 Jupiterimages Corporation; Washington, DC: Guinness World Records